Discipleship Junction

Stepping Up Stepping Out

Sheila Seifert and Beth Naylor

David C Cook

transforming lives together

STEPPING UP/STEPPING OUT
Published by David C. Cook
4050 Lee Vance View
Colorado Springs, CO 80918 U.S.A.

David C. Cook Distribution Canada
55 Woodslee Avenue, Paris, Ontario, Canada N3L 3E5

David C. Cook U.K., Kingsway Communications
Eastbourne, East Sussex BN23 6NT, England

David C. Cook and the graphic circle C logo
are registered trademarks of Cook Communications Ministries.

Written by Sheila Seifert and Beth Naylor
Cover Design: Scott Johnson/BMB Design
Cover Illustration: Scott Johnson/BMB Design
Interior Design: Sandy Flewelling/TrueBlue Design
Interior Illustrations: Aline Heiser

ISBN 978-0-7814-4562-7

First Printing 2008
Printed in the United States

2 3 4 5 6 7 8 9 10 11

042109

Table of Contents

WELCOME TO
DISCIPLESHIP JUNCTION!

Discipleship Junction is an all-new program that harnesses the power of FUN to build young disciples through interaction with Bible truth and with each other.

A complete, multiage children's ministry program, *Discipleship Junction* is packed full of interactive stories and drama, Scripture memory, and themed snacks and activities that will engage every child! It is guaranteed effective because its principles and methods of instruction are teacher-tested and kid-approved!

Intensive student-teacher interaction within a learning community that is relational and supportive makes *Discipleship Junction* an ideal program for including children with disabilities. Hands-on learning activities are easily adapted to include all students. For more ideas about inclusion, an excellent resource is *Let All the Children Come to Me* by MaLesa Breeding, Ed.D.; Dana Hood, Ph.D.; and Jerry Whitworth, Ed.D. (Colorado Springs: David C.Cook, 2006).

PUTTING THE PIECES TOGETHER

Get Set. We know you're busy, so we provide a list of materials and what you'll need to prepare for your lesson. You'll also need a photocopy machine and some basic classroom supplies: paper, pencils, tape, crayons, markers, butcher paper, scissors, glue, and index cards. When you see this icon 🕰 allow a little extra prep time.

Kids love to dress up! Many of our Bible lessons use costume props from the Bible time dress-up box. This can be as simple as a box of items you gather from around the house or purchase inexpensively from a secondhand store. It could include: fake beard, swords, head cloths and brow bands, bathrobes, modern-day dress-up clothes, crowns, decorative chains and belts, etc.

Tickets Please! *(10 minutes).* Each week begins with an activity option to involve children while parents are dropping others off.
- The *Welcome Time Activity* will excite children's interest and help them connect with the Bible Truth for the week.

All Aboard for Bible Truth! *(20 minutes).* Whole-group, interactive Bible lessons invite students ages 6–11 to participate in the entire lesson. Whether it's role-playing Zacchaeus or running a feather relay, kids will be engaged in exciting, hands-on lessons. Pre- and post-lesson discussion times encourage children to talk about their own life experiences and tie their knowledge to the week's Bible Truth.
- *Use the Clues!* Practice is an important part of learning and helps us move information from short-term to long-term memory. *Stepping Up/Stepping Out* uses the exciting theme of a hiking expedition—complete with a Trekking backpack—to help children practice and apply what they have learned. At the end of every lesson you'll unpack the Trekking backpack to go over the lesson focus. In the weeks that follow, students are repeatedly challenged to remember the Bible Truths by revisiting the items they have unpacked along their journey.

Bible Memory Waypoint *(5 minutes).* Toe tappin' and finger snappin' ... there's nothing like the power of FUN to motivate children. Movement, rhythm, role-play make it easy for kids to hide God's Word in their hearts (Psalm 119:11).

Prayer Station (15 minutes). Small-group prayer time for children. Wow! What an idea! Children break into small groups of three to five with an adult helper—we call them StationMasters. Using reproducible instruction cards, adults guide children to explore and practice new prayer skills. Together they'll share concerns, praise God, and practice the four activities of prayer using the imPACT model: *Praise, Ask, Confess, Thank.*

(Optional) **Snack Stop and Activities** (10 minutes). Tied to the theme of the lesson, options are available for snacks and activities in which lesson truths are practiced and shared. Look for the throttle icon that shows the level of mess, energy, or noise required for the activity.

On the Fast Track! Reproducible take-home pages invite families to interact in and through fun activities and Bible memory.

Are you looking for an additional way to motivate young learners? *Discipleship Junction* includes an optional incentive program that rewards students for completing take-home pages. Children return a signed *On the Fast Track!* ticket and choose a prize from the treasure box. If you have a new student, you might welcome that child with the choice of a treasure too. Simply cover and decorate a large shoe box. Fill with inexpensive items such as you might find at a party store.

HOW TO GET STARTED

1. **Begin by recruiting StationMasters**—adult helpers who will guide children through the process of praying in small groups. Don't have enough adult volunteers? How about recruiting middle- or high-school students to shepherd a group? Also consider enlisting a few faithful

prayer partners who will commit to praying for your class weekly.

Plan to have a brief training session with your volunteers in which you'll explain how to use the imPACT model of prayer. Each week you'll give the StationMasters a reproducible instruction card with the day's prayer theme and prayer suggestions to use with children in a small group.

2. **Set up your room.** You'll need a big area for your large-group Bible teaching time. You'll also need to identify spaces for each of your small prayer groups. Don't forget that moving chairs and tables or moving groups to a hallway is always an option. And children are willing helpers!

3. **Photocopy reproducible letters** (see Resources) to StationMasters and parents. Mail these two or three weeks before you begin *Discipleship Junction.*

4. **Photocopy On the Fast Track! pages for each child and StationMaster Cards for each adult helper.** If you choose, make copies of the reproducibles for all the lessons ahead of time. This can save a last-minute scramble when time is tight!

5. **Prepare the Trekking backpack and gather your backpacking supplies.** Each week you will have one or more items in your backpack that relate to the lesson idea to be learned. After discussing the item, you will hang your weekly reminder on a tree branch for the weeks that follow. See Resources on pages 84–85 for suggestions on creating a fun area.

6. Gather and prepare your materials, set out your snacks, and you are ready to roll. So ... **FULL SPEED AHEAD! ALL ABOARD FOR DISCIPLESHIP JUNCTION!**

LESSON ONE: Getting to Give

Memory Verse:

A generous man will prosper; he who refreshes others will himself be refreshed **(Proverbs 11:25).**

*Note: Younger children may memorize the shorter version of this verse in **bold** print.*

Bible Basis:

Genesis 13;
Matthew 19:16–22

Bible Truth:

God gives me things so I can be generous with others.

You Will Need:

- ☐ *(Optional)* Bible time dress-up box
- ☐ Trekking backpack
- ☐ brown craft paper
- ☐ butcher paper
- ☐ Bibles
- ☐ cardstock
- ☐ packaged trail mix
- ☐ package of cookies
- ☐ set of new markers
- ☐ business-size white envelope
- ☐ pennies (2 per child)
- ☐ rope
- ☐ sheets
- ☐ scrap paper
- ☐ *On the Fast Track! #1* take-home paper
- ☐ *StationMaster Card #1*
- ☐ *(Optional)* treasure box
- ☐ *(Optional)* snack: trail-mix ingredients (oaten-ring cereal, chocolate-coated candy, raisins, dried fruit, pretzel sticks, mini crackers, etc.), large bowl, serving spoon, napkins or small cups
- ☐ *(Optional)* Activity #1: rope and sheets or short room dividers, wadded paper (4–6 wads per student)
- ☐ *(Optional)* Activity #2: trail-mix ingredients in separate bags, serving bowls, large serving spoons, cups or napkins

When you see this icon, it means preparation will take more than five minutes.

GET SET!

(Lesson Preparation)

- ◼ Print today's Bible memory verse on craft paper: **A generous man will prosper; he who refreshes others will himself be refreshed (Proverbs 11:25).** Hang the verse on the wall.
- ◼ Photocopy *On the Fast Track! #1* for each child.
- ◼ Photocopy *StationMaster Card #1* for each helper.
- ◼ Set out the Trekking backpack and *(optional)* treasure box.
- ◼ Write in thick marker on the white envelope: 5 tickets to _____ game (write the name of a favorite sports team in the blank).
- ◼ Make an 8½" x 11" sign on cardstock using a thick marker: "video game console."
- ◼ Place in the backpack the package of cookies; video game console sign; a handful of new, colorful markers; and the envelope. Set the zipped-up backpack at the story area.
- ◼ Set up snack or outside play activities if you include these items in your children's ministry.
- ◼ Tape butcher paper to a wall, if using the Welcome Time Activity.
- ◼ Secure a rope across the playing area at about head height of your tallest students just before playing Activity #1.
- ◼ Make compact paper wads of the scrap paper (about 4–6 wads per student) if using Activity #1.

TICKETS PLEASE!
(Welcome and Bible Connection)

■ **Objective:** *To excite children's interest and connect their own life experiences with the Bible Truth, children design a mural and talk about hikes they've taken.*

Welcome Time Activity: Take a Hike Mural

■ **Materials:** *butcher paper, markers or crayons, tape*

As children arrive, direct them to the wall where you have taped the butcher paper. Ask children to work together to create a place where they imagine they could hike, such as a forest or a mountain trail. Children can draw trees, rocks, animals, the trail, and other features. Talk with them about hikes they've taken and what they've brought with them.

Sharing Time and Bible Connection

■ **Materials:** *backpack with cookies, video game console sign, markers, and the envelope inside*
Introduce today's lesson with an object lesson and discussion. As you talk, give every child the opportunity to say something. Ask for four volunteers to stand in front of the class. Build drama by making a big production of opening the backpack and deciding what to take out. One by one, take out the four items and give one to each child. Try to give the items to the children to whom you think they would be valuable. By turn, ask each child holding an object:

■ **What are you going to do with your _____ (cookies, etc.)?** After each child answers, let the rest of the class offer ideas of what they would do with the item. After all four have had their turn, collect the items; volunteers can return to their seats.
■ **How many of our four volunteers said they would generously share what they had been given?**
■ **When was the last time you received something that you chose to share with others?**
■ **Why would you choose to be generous with your things?** (because God asks us to, it's the right thing to do, to show care to others, because others need it more than I do)

After this sharing time, help your students connect their discussion to the Bible story they are about to hear from Genesis 13; Matthew 19:16–22.

We all have lots of stuff. And all of it is from God in some way. God has given us toys and books, food and pets, and other things. And he's given them to us so we can be generous with others. Let's look at two Bible stories to see who was <u>generous with what God had given them</u>.

ALL ABOARD FOR BIBLE TRUTH
(Bible Discover and Learn Time)

Genesis 13; Matthew 19:16–22

- ◼ *Objective: Children will study Genesis 13 and Matthew 19 to discover why God desires us to be generous with the things he gives us.*
- ◼ *Materials: Bibles, pencils, paper, Bible time dress-up box (optional)*

Divide the class into two or four groups, with competent readers in each group. Assign each group one of the Bible texts: Genesis 13 or Matthew 19:16–22. Hand out Bibles, paper, and pencils. **We're going to find out for ourselves what choices we should make about our stuff to stay on the path to know and follow God.**

Have children read their passage in their group. Older children will help younger ones find the passage; all should follow along as one or more group members read it. Instruct groups to find out who is doing what in their passage. Ask them to prepare a one-minute skit of the passage, using as many group members as possible. Helpers can assist with ideas and skit practice. If desired, children can use the Bible time dress-up box for props and costumes. After a set amount of time, call the groups back together and let each present their skit. When all have performed, compliment their efforts.

Summarize the stories: **The Genesis story told how Abraham and Lot both had big herds of animals. There wasn't enough room for them to live next to each other. Abraham let Lot choose what area he would take for his herds and family. Lot took the better piece of land. Abraham took the second-best. But God gave Abraham much more than that piece of land. He told Abraham he would own all the countryside, as far as he could see, and he would also have a really big family. Both these promises came true and were wonderful gifts to Abraham.**

The story from Matthew is about a young rich man who talked to Jesus. This rich man had all that he wanted. But he knew he didn't have the truth of Jesus in his life. He asked Jesus what he needed to do to be a follower of Jesus. Jesus told him he needed to sell his things and give the money to the poor.

Jesus didn't mean the man had to be poor to have eternal life. But Jesus knew that the things this man had were more important to him than following Jesus. Anything that keeps us from obeying Jesus with all our hearts is an idol, and it's bad for us. This man lost out on taking the path of walking with God because he wanted to hold onto all his things for himself.

Which of these stories shows us the way to walking on the path with God? (Abraham and Lot) **Abraham was willing to be generous with the land God had given him. He's our example of <u>being generous with the things God has given us</u>.**

Use the Clues!
(Bible Review)

■ *Materials: Trekking backpack, packaged trail mix*

Okay, let's see what you remember.
■ **Why did Abraham let Lot choose a piece of land first?** (he was willing to be generous with the land)
■ **How did God show his approval of Abraham's choice?** (God promised him all the land he could see in every direction, he said Abraham would have lots of children and grandchildren)
■ **What caused the rich young man to walk away from Jesus with sadness?** (he wasn't willing to be generous with his things, his riches were too important to him to let go of in order to follow Jesus)
■ **How can we follow Abraham's example as we walk on God's path?** (don't be greedy, be willing to share what we have, be generous with whatever we have)

Ask a volunteer to open the backpack and take out the trail mix.
■ **How could trail mix be useful on a hike?** (food when you're hungry, healthy snack)
■ **How is this trail mix a reminder that God gives us things so we can be generous with others?** (we can share our snacks and other things with those around us)
Hang the trail mix on the tree branch or hiking bulletin board.

BIBLE MEMORY WAYPOINT
(Scripture Memory)

Proverbs 11:25

■ *Objective: Children will hide God's Word in their hearts for guidance, protection, and encouragement.*
■ *Materials: two pennies per child*

Read this week's memory verse from the craft paper. Point to each word as you read it:
A generous man will prosper; he who refreshes others will himself be refreshed (Proverbs 11:25).

Read the verse together a few times until it's familiar. Then play "Coin Exchange": Give each child two pennies. They'll walk around looking for someone to whom to give their money and the verse. When a child stops in front of another, he will hand that child his coins and say the verse. The other child will reciprocate, so each will again have a set of coins. Then they each will find someone new to exchange with. Play for a set amount of time. Play background music during the activity, if desired.

PRAYER STATION

- **Objective:** *Children will explore and practice prayer for themselves in small groups.*
- **Materials:** *Copies of* StationMaster Card #1 *for each adult or teen helper.*

Break into small groups of three to five children. Assign a teen or adult helper to each small group, and give each helper a copy of *StationMaster Card #1* (see Resources) with ideas for group discussion and prayer.

SNACK STOP: TRAIL MIX (Optional)

Note: Combine the snack with Activity #2 to illustrate the Bible Truth, or serve separately here.

- **Materials:** *trail-mix ingredients (oaten-ring cereal, chocolate-coated candy, raisins, dried fruit, pretzel sticks, mini crackers, etc.), large bowl, cups or napkins, serving spoon*

Have children help you combine the trail mix ingredients in a large bowl and serve it. *Note: Always be aware of children with food allergies and have another option on hand if necessary.*

APPLICATION

- **Objective:** *Children will have opportunities to show how the lesson works in their own lives through activities and take-home papers.*

Some children's ministries may allow children to play outside at this point. If yours does not, choose one of the following activities.

Freely Give Game

■ *Materials: rope and sheets or short room dividers, wadded paper (4–6 wads per student)*

String the rope across the middle of the play area and drape the sheets over it as a room divider, or place a room divider in the center of the area. Split the class into two groups, one on each side of the screen. Divide the paper wads evenly between the two sides. At your signal, each team tries to toss all the wads on their side over the divider to the other side. As wads come whizzing back, teams should quickly snatch them up and toss them back. Play for a set time (30 to 60 seconds). When you call time, judge which side had the least number of wads. That team wins for being the most generous to share their wads with the other group. Play as long as time allows or until energy depletes.

 ## Trail Mix-It-Up

■ *Materials: trail-mix ingredients in separate bags, serving bowls, serving spoons, cups or napkins*

Have children find partners (large class) or work individually (small class) to choose one trail-mix ingredient and pour it into a serving bowl. Once all the ingredients are set out individually, let the children take a cup and serve themselves from the bowls to create a personalized trail mix. Talk about how the many types of ingredients make the trail mix fun and tasty. If children had chosen to keep their ingredient to themselves, the trail mix would lose a little bit of flavor and choice. By being generous, they all made a treat that everyone can enjoy.

 ### ON THE FAST TRACK! *(Take-Home Papers)*

(Optional) Introduce the treasure box by asking: **Who would like to choose a prize from the treasure box?** Anticipate excited responses. Show *On the Fast Track!* take-home papers. **When you take this *On the Fast Track!* paper home each week and do the activities, your parents can sign the ticket that you finished the work. Bring the signed ticket back to choose a prize from the treasure box.** Distribute the take-home papers just before children leave.

LESSON TWO: God Thinks I'm Cool

God's opinion counts most!

Memory Verse:
Humble yourselves before the Lord, and he will lift you up (James 4:10).

Bible Basis:
Daniel 1; Acts 4:32—5:10

Bible Truth:
What God thinks of me is more important than what others think.

You Will Need:

- [ ] Trekking backpack
- [ ] craft paper
- [ ] small travel or hand mirror
- [ ] balloons, including some that are small or deformed
- [ ] Bibles
- [ ] *On the Fast Track! #2* take-home paper
- [ ] *StationMaster Card #2*
- [ ] *(Optional)* treasure box
- [ ] *(Optional)* snack: baby carrots, raisins, mini graham crackers
- [ ] *(Optional)* Activity #1: inflated balloons (at least 5 more than there are children), permanent markers
- [ ] *(Optional)* Activity #2: various colors of thick yarn, craft sticks, scissors, double-stick tape *(optional)*

GET SET!
(Lesson Preparation)

- ■ Print today's Bible memory verse on craft paper: **Humble yourselves before the Lord, and he will lift you up (James 4:10).** Hang the verse on the wall.
- ■ Photocopy *On the Fast Track! #2* for each child.
- ■ Photocopy *StationMaster Card #2* for each helper.
- ■ Set out the Trekking backpack and *(optional)* treasure box.
- ■ Photocopy the messages on Resources page 85, cut apart and insert into balloons before inflating, if using Activity #1.
- ■ Place the mirror in the backpack. Set the zipped-up backpack at the story area.
- ■ Set up snack or outside play activities if you include these items in your children's ministry.

TICKETS PLEASE!
(Welcome and Bible Connection)

- ■ *Objective: To excite children's interest and connect their own life experiences with the Bible Truth, children will talk about what makes someone "cool."*

When you see this icon, it means preparation will take more than five minutes.

Welcome Time Activity: Who Am I?

■ *Materials:* pencils and paper

As children arrive, direct them to the helper who is interacting with the early arrivals. Children will each quickly whisper something about themselves to the helper, who will write it down. Their fact can be about their family, their hobbies, what they like or don't like to eat or do, something from their younger childhood (a pet, trip, experience, fear). Once the helper has collected several facts, he'll mix them up and then read one. Children will try to guess who said it. Helper can interject that no matter what you're like and where you're from, you're cool in God's eyes.

Sharing Time and Bible Connection

Introduce today's lesson by discussing these questions with your students. As you talk, give every child the opportunity to say something.

■ **Can you think of a time you did something to make another person like you or think you were cool or special?**

■ **What things do people do so they will look good in someone else's eyes?** (brag about what they have, show off, act tough, make fun of others)

■ **What does it matter whether we do things for the approval of people like our friends?** (it matters a lot, because if we're trying to show off or look good for people, we probably aren't paying attention to what God thinks of our attitudes, behavior, or reasons for doing something)

After this sharing time, help your students connect their discussion to the Bible story they are about to hear from Daniel 1 and Acts 4—5.

Sometimes we do or say things to show off to people around us. We might decide to do something or not do something because our friends will like us or be impressed by us. But what matters is <u>what God thinks of us. His opinion of us is the most important</u>. Three people in the Bible are good examples of this. Let's investigate.

ALL ABOARD FOR BIBLE TRUTH
(Bible Discover and Learn Time)   Daniel 1; Acts 4:32–5:10

■ *Objective:* Children will study Daniel 1 and Acts 4—5 to compare how Daniel acted versus how Ananias and Sapphira acted and whose opinion they valued most.
■ *Materials:* Bibles, pencils, paper, Trekking backpack with mirror inside

Divide the class into two or four groups, with competent readers in each group. Assign each group one of the Bible texts: Daniel 1 or Acts 4:32—5:10. Hand out Bibles, paper, and pencils. **Let's look to see what matters more: other people's opinions of us or God's.**

Have children read their passage in their group. Older children will help younger ones find the passage; all should follow along as one or more group members read it. Instruct groups to find out who is doing what in their passage. When they've had time to read the text and discuss it, ask one volunteer from the Daniel passage and one from the Acts passage to tell the main points of their story. Encourage the rest of the class to cheer for the Bible characters who cared about what God thought of them, and boo at the characters who cared more about what other people thought. Helpers should stimulate energetic cheering and booing as needed.

Summarize the two stories: **In Daniel 1, a young Jewish man named Daniel and other Jewish young men were being trained as assistants of the king of Babylon. The king wanted the men to eat his special food. But God had commanded the Jews not to eat many things that the king liked. So Daniel and three friends who cared what God thought asked for different food. The king's official let them try eating this different food, and God showed them favor and blessed them. They were healthier and happier than those who ate the king's special food. God gave the four men 10 times as much special knowledge and wisdom than the others who were serving the king, because they had done what they knew God wanted, instead of what everyone else was doing.**

In Acts, a group of believers shared all their belongings so everyone would have the same things. Some sold their land to help those who had less money. One man and his wife decided to sell their land. When they presented the money to the rest of the church, they pretended to give all of it. But they secretly kept some for themselves. They wanted to look like they were very generous so others would be impressed. But God's Spirit told the church leaders what Ananias and Sapphira had done, and their lie was made public. God punished them for lying about giving to him.

Which of these stories shows us whose opinion counts more: God's or others'? (Daniel) **Daniel knew that <u>what God thought of him was more important then even what a king would think of him</u>.** He's our example of how to follow God on the right path.

Use the Clues!
(Bible Review)

- **Materials:** *Trekking backpack, mirror*

Okay, let's see what you remember.
- **Why didn't Daniel and his three friends want to eat the king's special foods?** (because it was food God had told the Jews not to eat)
- **How did God show his approval of Daniel's choice?** (he made the four men more wise and knowledgeable and healthier and stronger than the others who ate the king's food)
- **Why were some of the Christians in the book of Acts selling land?** (to help out the Christians who didn't have money)
- **Why was God not pleased with Ananias and Sapphira's gift of money?** (they kept part of it back for themselves but lied about it and acted like they were giving all their money, they wanted others to think they were generous so they tried to fool the church leaders)
- **In what ways should we be most concerned with what God thinks of us?** Allow reasonable responses.

Ask a volunteer to open the backpack and take out the mirror.
- **How could a mirror be useful if you're hiking?** (you can use it to signal for help by flashing it in the sun)
- **How is this mirror a reminder that what God thinks of us is the most important?** (it reminds us to think of how God sees us, and not what other people are seeing)

Hang the mirror on the tree branch or hiking bulletin board. Review the previous lesson by asking a volunteer to explain what the trail mix stands for (God gives us things so we can be generous with others, we should share what we have instead of wanting more for ourselves).

BIBLE MEMORY WAYPOINT
(Scripture Memory)

James 4:10

- **Objective:** *Children will hide God's Word in their hearts for guidance, protection, and encouragement.*

Read this week's memory verse from the craft paper. Point to each word as you read it:
Humble yourselves before the Lord, and he will lift you up (James 4:10).
Explain that to be humble means to not think of yourself as better than other people. Add actions to help children memorize the verse. As you say "humble yourselves," lead children in kneeling down. For "lift you up," direct the kids to stand up and lift their arms. Ask for volunteers to lead the class in practicing the verse with the actions (including the reference).

PRAYER STATION

- ■ *Objective: Children will explore and practice prayer for themselves in small groups.*
- ■ *Materials: Copies of StationMaster Card #2 for each adult or teen helper*

Break into small groups of three to five children. Assign a teen or adult helper to each small group and give each helper a copy of *StationMaster Card #2* (see Resources) with ideas for group discussion and prayer.

SNACK STOP: HEALTHY AND HEARTY (Optional)

If you plan to provide a snack, this is an ideal time to serve it.

- ■ *Materials: baby carrots, raisins, mini graham crackers*

God gave the Jews in Daniel's time laws about food to eat and not eat. When Jesus came, he said those laws no longer apply. Does that mean we're free to have just sweets and snacks? How about eating stuff our friends think is cool, like a certain brand of soda or chips? God wants us to have healthy bodies and strong minds. That's why we should eat lots of different foods. Offer baby carrots, raisins, and mini graham crackers. As the children eat, engage them in conversation about other ways they realize they should make decisions based on what God thinks instead of people.

Note: Always be aware of children with food allergies and have another option on hand if necessary.

APPLICATION

- ■ *Objective: Children will have opportunities to show how the lesson works in their own lives through activities and take-home papers.*

Some children's ministries may allow children to play outside at this point. If yours does not, choose one of the following activities.

Balloon Relay

■ *Materials: inflated balloons (at least five more than there are children) with papers inside (some balloons should be smaller than others or deformed), permanent markers*

Invite the children to choose an inflated balloon. Give them two minutes to draw designs on their balloons to make them the best-looking balloons they can. Have children put their balloons in a cluster. At your signal, they should run to the cluster, grab a balloon, and pop it however they can. Have them read (older children can read for younger ones) the paper inside their balloons. Point out that the messages in the smaller or deformed balloons were just as special as those inside the fancy balloons.

Remember that how you look on the outside to others is not as important as what God thinks of you.

 In God's Eyes

■ *Materials: various colors of thick yarn, craft sticks, scissors, double-stick tape (optional)*

Create a cross with the craft sticks, so they are touching in the middles of both sticks. Use a small piece of double-stick tape, if desired, to hold the sticks in position. Take one end of a yarn length and wrap over and around one stick, then over and around the next, moving in a circular direction. To change colors of yarn, cut and tie on a new color in a tight knot, then continue. Wrap yarn until the sticks are almost concealed. Cut the yarn and tuck the loose end into the weaving.

Explain that this creation is called a God's Eye and it is a reminder that who we are in his eyes is most important.

 ON THE FAST TRACK! *(Take-Home Papers)*

(Optional) Introduce the treasure box by asking: **Who would like to choose a prize from the treasure box?** Anticipate excited responses. Show *On the Fast Track!* take-home papers. **When you take this *On the Fast Track!* paper home each week and do the activities, your parents can sign the ticket that you finished the work. Bring the signed ticket back to choose a prize from the treasure box.** Distribute the take-home papers just before children leave.

Godly wisdom is best!

Memory Verse:

The fear of the LORD is the beginning of wisdom; all who follow his precepts have good understanding **(Psalm 111:10).**

Note: Younger children may memorize the shorter version of this verse in bold print.

Bible Basis:

Genesis 4:1–12;
2 Chronicles 1:1–12

Bible Truth:

Having godly wisdom is better than being right all the time.

You Will Need:

- [ ] Trekking backpack
- [ ] craft paper
- [ ] compass
- [ ] Bibles
- [ ] envelope
- [ ] *(Optional)* small prizes
- [ ] *On the Fast Track! #3* take-home paper
- [ ] *StationMaster Card #3*
- [ ] *(Optional)* treasure box
- [ ] *(Optional)* snack: large round crackers, rice cakes or mini bagel halves, pretzel sticks, flavored cream cheese or frosting, plastic knives
- [ ] *(Optional)* Activity #1: long piece of sturdy rope or circular tug-of-war rope, bandanna, masking tape
- [ ] *(Optional)* Activity #2: cardstock, paper fastener, rulers, markers, large paper clips

When you see this icon, it means preparation will take more than five minutes.

GET SET!
(Lesson Preparation)

- ■ ⏱ Print today's Bible memory verse on craft paper: **The fear of the LORD is the beginning of wisdom; all who follow his precepts have good understanding (Psalm 111:10).** Hang the verse on the wall.
- ■ Photocopy *On the Fast Track! #3* for each child.
- ■ Photocopy *StationMaster Card #3* for each helper.
- ■ ⏱ Handwrite the "advice" letter from the resources page on a slip of paper and insert in an envelope.
- ■ Set out the Trekking backpack and *(optional)* treasure box.
- ■ Create two tape lines in the center of the playing area, three feet apart, if using Activity #1.
- ■ Place the compass in the backpack. Set the zipped-up backpack at the story area.
- ■ Set up snack or outside play activities if you include these items in your children's ministry.

TICKETS PLEASE!
(Welcome and Bible Connection)

- ■ **Objective:** *To excite children's interest and connect their own life experiences with the Bible Truth, children will play a game to practice discerning right answers.*

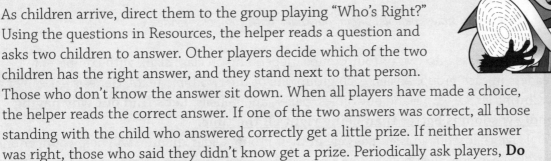

Welcome Time Activity: Who's Right?

■ *Materials: questions from Resources pages 86–87, small prizes (candies, stickers, etc.)*

As children arrive, direct them to the group playing "Who's Right?" Using the questions in Resources, the helper reads a question and asks two children to answer. Other players decide which of the two children has the right answer, and they stand next to that person. Those who don't know the answer sit down. When all players have made a choice, the helper reads the correct answer. If one of the two answers was correct, all those standing with the child who answered correctly get a little prize. If neither answer was right, those who said they didn't know get a prize. Periodically ask players, **Do you think you can be right all the time?**

Sharing Time and Bible Connection

■ *Materials: advice letter in envelope (Resources page 88)*

Introduce today's lesson with this object lesson and discussion. As you talk, give every child the opportunity to say something.

Ask a competent reader to read out loud the letter you hand him or her. Then discuss:

■ **What do you think this person should do?**
■ **Can you think of a time when you thought your plan or idea was the best, but it didn't turn out that way?**
■ **When you think your way is best and someone else has a different idea, how do you decide which way is best?**

After this sharing time, help your students connect their discussion to the Bible story they are about to hear from Genesis 4 and 2 Chronicles 1.

We all want to be right. It's hard to accept that someone else can have a better plan or know more about a situation. Thinking that our own way is always the right one is a trap we can easily fall into. What's better to remember is that <u>having godly wisdom is better than always being right</u>. Two guys in the Old Testament are examples for us to learn from. Let's learn more about them.

ALL ABOARD FOR BIBLE TRUTH
(Bible Discover and Learn Time)   Genesis 4:1–12; 2 Chronicles 1:1–12

■ **Objective:** *Children will study Genesis 4 and 2 Chronicles 1 to find out who used godly wisdom.*
■ **Materials:** *Bibles, pencils, paper, backpack with compass inside*

Divide the class into two or four groups (depending on class size), with competent readers in each group. Assign each group one of the two Bible texts: Genesis 4:1–12 or 2 Chronicles 1:1–12. Hand out Bibles, paper, and pencils. **Let's find out why <u>having godly wisdom is better than being right all the time</u>.**

Have children read their passage in their group. Older children will help younger ones find the passage; all should follow along as one or more group members read it. Instruct groups to find out who is doing what in their passage. When they've had time to read the text, have them choose words and phrases that describe the person in the text. A group scribe (or helper, if needed) will write the words and phrases on paper, but not list the character's name. Ask one volunteer from each group to share their list. After all lists have been shared, ask who is described by each list.

Summarize the two stories: **Cain was a farmer. His brother, Abel, raised animals. They both brought offerings to God from what they raised. Abel brought some of his best animals, and God accepted this offering. But Cain's offering wasn't acceptable to God. We don't know exactly why. Cain didn't like that his offering wasn't good in God's eyes. He couldn't admit that he wasn't right with what he had done. Cain was mad and not willing to change his mind, even after God told him he could do what was right so his offering could be acceptable. Cain let his anger control him, and he killed his brother. Being right was more important to Cain than pleasing God.**

In 2 Chronicles, we find out that Solomon was David's son. He had a huge kingdom and lots of servants. He was rich and powerful. But Solomon didn't use that power to make people do things his way. When God said Solomon could ask for whatever he wanted, Solomon only wanted wisdom. He wanted to know how to make choices that would please and honor God. His desire was to be a wise and good leader. He knew he couldn't be the best leader for the people on his own. <u>Solomon showed us that having godly wisdom is better than being right all the time</u>. He's our example of how to follow God on the right path.

Use the Clues!
(Bible Review)

■ **Materials:** *Trekking backpack, compass*

Okay, let's see what you remember.

■ **What made Cain so mad he killed his brother?** (God didn't accept his offering because it wasn't done right, Cain didn't like that God said he wasn't right)

■ **What could Cain have done differently?** (apologized to God, made his offering the kind God would accept, be willing to admit he wasn't right)

■ **Why would Solomon ask for wisdom if he was already the king?** (he knew he needed godly wisdom, not his own, to rule wisely; he knew he wouldn't always be right)

■ **How can we use these examples in our own lives?** (not try to be right all the time, admit when you're wrong, ask God for wisdom and use it, learn to know God better so you can know his wisdom)

Ask a volunteer to open the backpack and take out the compass.

■ **How could a compass be useful if you're hiking?** (it shows you which way is north, helps you go in the right direction)

■ **How is this compass a reminder that having godly wisdom is more important than being right all the time?** (the compass points to the right direction like godly wisdom can help us go the right way, instead of trying to be right on our own)

Hang the compass on the tree branch or hiking bulletin board. Review the previous lessons by asking volunteers to explain what the other hanging items stand for. (See Resources pages 84–85 for the meaning of the backpack items.)

BIBLE MEMORY WAYPOINT
(Scripture Memory)

Psalm 111:10

■ **Objective:** *Children will hide God's Word in their hearts for guidance, protection, and encouragement.*

Read this week's memory verse from the poster. Point to each word as you read it:

The fear of the LORD is the beginning of wisdom; all who follow his precepts have good understanding (Psalm 111:10).

To help children memorize the Bible verse, put it to a snappy rhythm.

The fear (clap, clap)
of the LORD (clap, clap)
is the beginning (clap, clap)
of wisdom (clap, clap).

Then walk in a quick circle with the children behind you, saying the rest of the verse and reference. Recruit some volunteers to lead the clapping and following the rhythm until the verse is familiar.

PRAYER STATION

- **Objective:** *Children will explore and practice prayer for themselves in small groups.*
- **Materials:** *Copies of* StationMaster Card #3 *for each adult or teen helper*

Break into small groups of three to five children. Assign a teen or adult helper to each small group and give each helper a copy of *StationMaster Card #3* (see Resources) with ideas for group discussion and prayer.

SNACK STOP: CRUNCHABLE COMPASSES (Optional)

If you plan to provide a snack, this is an ideal time to serve it.

- **Materials:** *large round crackers, rice cakes or mini bagel halves, pretzel sticks, flavored cream cheese or frosting, plastic knives*

Children will create compasses. Have children lightly spread frosting or cream cheese on one side of the cracker or bagel. For the four directional pointers, have them break two pretzel sticks in half and lay the four pieces at right angles for the four compass points. The sticks should poke out from the edges of the base. Talk about situations the children have experienced where they wanted to be right, and how godly wisdom could have been used.

Note: Always be aware of children with food allergies and have another option on hand if necessary.

APPLICATION

- **Objective:** *Children will have opportunities to show how the lesson works in their own lives through activities and take-home papers.*

Some children's ministries may allow children to play outside at this point. If yours does not, choose one of the following activities.

 Tug of War

- **Materials:** *long piece of sturdy rope or circular tug-of-war rope, bandanna, masking tape*

Divide the class into small teams of three to five children on each team (you'll need at least two teams). Two teams can play at a time. Remaining teams can cheer for the players until their turn. Lay the tug-of-war rope in the center of the playing area with the bandanna centered between the two lines. The opposing teams will take hold of their side of the rope. At your signal, each team tries to pull the other team toward them. A team wins when the bandanna crosses the team's line. Ask children: **How is this game like trying to always be right?** (when no one wants to give in or use godly wisdom, people can pull and struggle against each other)

 My Way or the Wise Way Spinner

- **Materials:** *cardstock, paper fastener, rulers, markers, large paper clips*

Children will make a spinner as a reminder to use godly wisdom when they are tempted to push their way on others. Show children how to divide the paper into four sections; draw lines with a thick black marker to separate the sections. Place the paper clip on the paper fastener, and push the paper fastener through the center of the paper, securing on the back side. The clip is the spinner pointer. In the four sections, have children write or draw their options when they are tempted to stubbornly insist on their own way in a situation. Ideas: write "ask God for his wisdom," "say nothing," "let the other person have their way," "ask another person for their idea."

 ON THE FAST TRACK! *(Take-Home Papers)*

(Optional) Introduce the treasure box by asking: **Who would like to choose a prize from the treasure box?** Anticipate excited responses. Show *On the Fast Track!* take-home papers. **When you take this *On the Fast Track!* paper home each week and do the activities, your parents can sign the ticket that you finished the work. Bring the signed ticket back to choose a prize from the treasure box.** Distribute the take-home papers just before children leave.

LESSON FOUR: Walking the Fair Way

Memory Verse:
Blessed are they who maintain justice, who constantly do what is right (Psalm 106:3).

Bible Basis:
1 Samuel 2:12–17, 22–25, 27–35; 4:10–11; 1 Kings 3:16–28

Bible Truth:
God's justice shows me what is fair.

God's way is just!

You Will Need:
- [ ] Trekking backpack
- [ ] craft paper
- [ ] binoculars
- [ ] twine
- [ ] two shallow boxes
- [ ] ruler or dowel
- [ ] candy or balloons
- [ ] Bibles
- [ ] black marker
- [ ] large chalkboard
- [ ] chalk
- [ ] *On the Fast Track! #4* take-home paper
- [ ] *StationMaster Card #4*
- [ ] *(Optional)* treasure box
- [ ] *(Optional)* snack: prepared cubed fruit-flavored gelatin, paper cups, spoons
- [ ] *(Optional)* Activity #1: "FAIR" and "UNFAIR" signs, fair and unfair situation ideas (see Resources page 89)
- [ ] *(Optional)* Activity #2: large sheets of cardstock, markers

 When you see this icon, it means preparation will take more than five minutes.

 ## GET SET!
(Lesson Preparation)

- ■ Print today's Bible memory verse on craft paper: **Blessed are they who maintain justice, who constantly do what is right (Psalm 106:3).** Hang the verse on the wall.
- ■ Photocopy *On the Fast Track! #4* for each child.
- ■ Photocopy *StationMaster Card #4* for each helper.
- ■ Set out the Trekking backpack and *(optional)* treasure box.
- ■ Make two signs: write "FAIR" and "UNFAIR" in thick black marker on sheets of paper, and post on opposite sides of the play area, if using Activity #1.
- ■ If serving gelatin for the snack, prepare the day before and refrigerate, then cut into cubes before class begins.
- ■ Place the binoculars in the backpack. Set the zipped-up backpack at the story area.
- ■ Make a scale by punching a hole in each of the four sides of both shallow boxes. Push a piece of twine through holes on opposite sides and knot to hold in place; do the same on the other set of holes. Repeat for second box. Tie one end of a 6" twine piece to the hangers of one box; repeat with another 6" length and the other box. Tie each remaining end of the 6" twine to one end of a ruler.

TICKETS PLEASE!
(Welcome and Bible Connection)

- ■ *Objective: To excite children's interest and connect their own life experiences with the Bible Truth, children will play with a fairness scale and talk about their ideas about fairness and justice.*

Welcome Time Activity: Fairness Scale

■ *Materials: scale made before class (see **Get Set!**)*
   As children arrive, they can join a group experimenting with the homemade scale. Children can take turns finding small items around the room to set in the two sides of the scale and see if they balance each other. Ask children to predict which side will be heavier (lower), and challenge them to find items that will be the same weight and so balance each other. Talk about how a scale is a symbol for justice and how justice is related to fairness.

Sharing Time and Bible Connection

■ *Materials: scale from the Welcome Time Activity, balloons or candy*

Introduce today's lesson by discussing these questions with your students. As you talk, give every child the opportunity to say something.

■ **What is justice?** (fairness in the way people are treated or decisions are made)
■ **Justice and fairness are closely connected. When have you had an experience with fairness?** Allow for responses.
■ **How does this scale give us a picture of justice and fairness?** (when the two sides are the same level, the things in the two sides of the scale are equal, they balance; when someone is treated fairly, what they get or do is the same as what someone else gets or does)
■ **If I was going to give this handful of candy/balloons to** _____ (child's name), **and I wanted to be fair about giving the same amount to** _____ (another child's name), **how would the scale help?** Place a handful of wrapped candies or uninflated balloons on one side of the scale. Use children's suggestions to end up with an equal amount of goodies in the opposite side.
■ **How can you tell if someone is acting fairly or justly?** (when they make a decision or act in a way that gives everyone the same treatment, when someone gets what they deserve)

   After this sharing time, help your students connect their discussion to the Bible story they are about to hear from 1 Samuel 2 and 4 and 1 Kings 3.
   People have lots of ideas about what is fair. But the only true fairness is based on God's justice. God is always totally fair and just. He always gives each of us the same amount of love, the same forgiveness when we confess our sins, and the same promise of heaven one day. Let's see how some people in the Bible experienced how <u>**God's justice shows us what is fair.**</u>

ALL ABOARD FOR BIBLE TRUTH
(Bible Discover and Learn Time)

1 Samuel 2:12-17, 22-25, 27-35; 4:10-11; 1 Kings 3:16-28

- **Objective:** *Children will study 1 Samuel 2 and 4 and 1 Kings 3 to find out how Eli's sons received justice for wrongdoing and Solomon executed godly justice in a dispute.*
- **Materials:** *Bibles, Trekking backpack with binoculars inside*

Divide the class into two or four groups (depending on class size), with competent readers in each group. Assign each group one of the Bible texts: 1 Samuel 2:12–17, 22–25, 27–35; 4:10–11 or 1 Kings 3:16–28. Hand out Bibles. **Let's find out how God's justice is always fair.**

Explain that the children will read their passage as a group. After they've had time to read it and understand what's going on, they're going to perform freeze frames of their passage. Older children should help younger ones find the passage; all should follow along as one or more group members read it. Instruct groups to find out who is doing what in their passage.

Once the groups have finished reading, bring everyone together. You'll read the passage out loud as narrator. At three strategic places in each passage, pause. Some of the group members will spontaneously create a freeze frame (frozen dramatic picture) of what you just read. Helpers can assist as needed. If more than one group has read the same passage, alternate so every group has a chance to participate. It's possible not all students will be in a freeze frame, but encourage them to try to include everyone. Do this for both passages.

Stop for a freeze frame after these verses in 1 Samuel: 1 Samuel 2:14; 1 Samuel 2:28; 1 Samuel 4:10–11. Stop after these verses in 1 Kings: 1 Kings 3:16; 1 Kings 3:22; 1 Kings 3:26.

Summarize the two stories: **Eli was a priest of God in the Old Testament. He had two grown-up sons who were also priests, but they did wrong things and didn't honor God at all. They made God very angry by not following his rules for sacrifices. They were not living right. Eli knew his sons were dishonoring God. He told them to stop, but they wouldn't listen. So God had to deal justly with these young men for their terrible actions and desire to do wrong. God caused the two sons to be killed in a battle with Israel's enemies. Because the two young men didn't honor God and act according to his law, God justly gave them what they deserved.**

King Solomon also had to make choices about fairness and justice. As king he had to judge the actions of the people when they disagreed or argued. Last week we learned how Solomon asked God for wisdom, and God gave him all he needed. In this story, Solomon had to use godly wisdom to figure out who the baby's real mother was. Both women said the baby was theirs. Solomon found a fair way to find out the truth and provide justice to the real mother.

We all want to have people be fair with us. Because of sin, there is lots of unfairness, and life can be very unjust. <u>We will be able to be fair and live justly when we ask God to show us his justice</u>.

Use the Clues!
(Bible Review)

Okay, let's see what you remember.

■ **How were Eli's sons dishonoring God?** (taking food from the sacrifice meant for God, taking advantage of their jobs as priests)

■ **How did God show justice toward them?** (they were killed in a battle with the Philistines)

■ **What problem of fairness did Solomon have to work out?** (which mother a baby really belonged to)

■ **How did Solomon use God's justice to be fair in his decision?** (he used godly wisdom, he did what God would want done so the true mother would get her baby back)

■ **What are some situations where you can use godly justice?** Allow for responses.

Ask a volunteer to open the backpack and take out the binoculars.

■ **How would binoculars be useful for hiking?** (they help you see something far away, you could spot birds, see what's at the top of a hill, or maybe find someone who's lost)

■ **How are these binoculars a reminder that having God's justice shows us what's fair?** (like binoculars bring faraway things into view, God's justice brings fairness into clear view, we can see fairness the right way by seeing things from God's idea of justice)

Hang the binoculars on the tree branch or hiking bulletin board. Review the previous lessons by asking volunteers to explain what the other hanging items stand for. (See Resources for the meaning of the backpack items.)

BIBLE MEMORY WAYPOINT   Psalm 106:3
(Scripture Memory)

■ *Objective: Children will hide God's Word in their hearts for guidance, protection, and encouragement.*

Read this week's memory verse from the craft paper. Point to each word as you read it:

Blessed are they who maintain justice, who constantly do what is right (Psalm 106:3).

After rehearsing the verse several times, play a game to cement the verse in children's memories. Have two or more teams line up behind a line at least 10 feet from a large whiteboard or chalkboard. Helpers should stand at the board between teams to screen the writing from other teams and to help younger children with writing. When you say "Go!" one player from each team runs to the board, picks up the marker or chalk and writes the first word of the verse, then runs back. Successive team members add words one by one. Helpers standing at the board can have younger children whisper the word in their ear and then write it for them. They can also prompt players who write the wrong word.

PRAYER STATION

- **Objective:** *Children will explore and practice prayer for themselves in small groups.*
- **Materials:** *Copies of* StationMaster Card #4 *for each adult or teen helper*

Break into small groups of three to five children. Assign a teen or adult helper to each small group, and give each helper a copy of *StationMaster Card #4* (see Resources) with ideas for group discussion and prayer.

SNACK STOP: JUSTICE JIGGLERS (Optional)

If you plan to provide a snack, this is an ideal time to serve it.

- **Materials:** *cubed fruit-flavored gelatin, paper cups, spoons*

Serve children cubes of gelatin in cups. Talk about how justice and fairness that don't agree with God's justice can be as unsteady and changing as jiggly gelatin. Ask children for examples of fairness that don't match God's justice and why this kind of fairness can be unsteady and hurtful.

Note: Always be aware of children with food allergies and have another option on hand if necessary.

APPLICATION

- **Objective:** *Children will have opportunities to show how the lesson works in their own lives through activities and take-home papers.*

Some children's ministries may allow children to play outside at this point. If yours does not, choose one of the following activities.

Fair/Unfair

■ **Materials:** *"FAIR" and "UNFAIR" signs, fair and unfair situation ideas*

Point out the two signs on opposite sides of the room and read them for non-readers. You'll give a statement, and children will choose whether to run to the FAIR or UNFAIR side. They should be prepared to defend their choice by stating why they made that choice. For unfair statements, ask children to tell how the statement could be made fair.

Poster

■ **Materials:** *large sheets of cardstock, markers*

Give children an opportunity to create a poster that shows what they've learned today about God's justice and fairness. Possibilities: illustrate part of one of the Bible stories, draw a situation that shows justice and fairness, draw a scale, or write the Bible Truth and decorate it.

ON THE FAST TRACK! *(Take-Home Papers)*

(Optional) Introduce the treasure box by asking: **Who would like to choose a prize from the treasure box?** Anticipate excited responses. Show *On the Fast Track!* take-home papers. **When you take this *On the Fast Track!* paper home each week and do the activities, your parents can sign the ticket that you finished the work. Bring the signed ticket back to choose a prize from the treasure box.** Distribute the take-home papers just before children leave.

Memory Verse:

Obey me, and I will be your God and you will be my people. **Walk in all the ways I command you, that it may go well with you (Jeremiah 7:23).**

Note: Younger children may memorize the shorter version of this verse in bold print.

Bible Basis:

1 Samuel 15:1–23;
Genesis 6:9—7:24

Bible Truth:

Choosing God's way is better than choosing my way.

God's Way Is Best!

You Will Need:

- ☐ Trekking backpack
- ☐ Bible time dress-up box
- ☐ craft paper
- ☐ 2 maps
- ☐ Bibles
- ☐ *On the Fast Track! #5* take-home paper
- ☐ *StationMaster Card #5*
- ☐ *(Optional)* treasure box
- ☐ *(Optional)* snack: large pretzel rods, chocolate syrup, caramel ice-cream topping, fruit-flavored syrup, apple butter, paper plates
- ☐ *(Optional)* Activity #1: boxes, chairs, rope, hula hoop, buckets or small, clean trash cans
- ☐ *(Optional)* Activity #2: paper cups or blocks

When you see this icon, it means preparation will take more than five minutes.

GET SET!
(Lesson Preparation)

- ◼ ⏱ Print today's Bible memory verse on craft paper: **Obey me, and I will be your God and you will be my people. Walk in all the ways I command you, that it may go well with you (Jeremiah 7:23).** Hang the verse on the wall.
- ◼ Photocopy *On the Fast Track! #5* for each child.
- ◼ Photocopy *StationMaster Card #5* for each helper.
- ◼ ⏱ Make a memory verse puzzle from one map. (For a large class, you might want to make more than one for more hands-on time for the students.) Write the memory verse on the map in thick marker so it can be easily read. Cut the map into 12 or more pieces (depending on map size). Hide the pieces around the room.
- ◼ Set out the Trekking backpack and *(optional)* treasure box.
- ◼ Set up snack or outside play activities if you include these items in your children's ministry.
- ◼ Place the map in the backpack. Set the zipped-up backpack at the story area.
- ◼ For next week's Bible story, recruit two men (teens or older) to play the parts of the rich man who dies (Luke 16:19–31) and John the Baptist (Mark 1:4–8). Ask them to become very familiar with their Scripture texts so you can interview them as their characters next week.

TICKETS PLEASE!
(Welcome and Bible Connection)

- ◼ *Objective: To excite children's interest and connect their own life experiences with the Bible Truth, children will play a game and consider why they shouldn't always have their own way.*

Welcome Time Activity: Follow the Leader

As children arrive, direct them to where a helper is overseeing a game of Follow the Leader. The helper can start the game by leading the children around the room in various modes: walking backward, skipping, hopping, crowing like a rooster, etc. After each circuit is done, change leaders so children have a chance to lead. Talk with children about why they don't go their own way instead of following the leader.

Sharing Time and Bible Connection

Introduce today's lesson by discussing these questions with your students. As you talk, give every child the opportunity to say something.

- **Have you gone for a hike or walk and decided not to follow the signs or map? What happened?**
- **Share a time you chose to do something your own way, even when an adult wanted you to do it differently.**
- **What difference could a map or some signs make when you need to choose the best way to travel?** (get to the destination in shorter time, not get lost, not face danger, be safe, find good things along the way)

After this sharing time, help your students connect their discussion to the Bible story they are about to hear from 1 Samuel 15 and Genesis 6—7.

Have you watched little kids who are just learning to walk? They want to go the way they choose. Their mom or dad wants them to walk a certain direction, but the toddler sometimes wants to go another way. We're like that too. God has a way for us to walk and to live, but as humans we often want to go our own way. What happens when we stubbornly choose our own way and ignore God's way? Two Bible people can show us why <u>choosing God's way is better than choosing our own way</u>.

ALL ABOARD FOR BIBLE TRUTH   1 Samuel 15:1–23; Genesis 6:9–7:24
(Bible Discover and Learn Time)

■ *Objective: Children will study 1 Samuel 15 and Genesis 6—7 to learn how Saul followed his own way and suffered, while Noah chose God's way and was blessed.*

■ *Materials: Bibles, Bible time dress-up box, Trekking backpack with map inside*

Divide the class into two or four groups (depending on class size), with competent readers in each group. Assign each group one of the Bible texts: 1 Samuel 15:1–23 or Genesis 6:9—7:24. Hand out Bibles. **Let's find out why <u>choosing God's way is better than choosing our own way</u>.**

Have children read their passage in their group. Older children will help younger ones find the passage; all should follow along as one or more group members read it. After they've read the passage, the groups should create a short drama of the story. Provide the Bible time dress-up box for costume choices.

After groups have presented their dramas, summarize the stories: **God commanded King Saul to lead his Israelite army to fight the Amalekites. He told Saul to destroy everything, even the animals. Saul defeated the enemy, but he took their king captive and kept the best of their animals and possessions. Saul decided to only destroy the ugly and worthless belongings. God was angry with Saul for choosing his own way instead of following God's commands. Because Saul chose to go his own way, and not God's, Saul would lose his job as the king of Israel.**

Noah also had a chance to follow his own way or do things God's way. God gave Noah a gigantic job: to build a huge boat—in a place where there was no water to float it! Noah didn't ask God why; he just got busy with his sons to construct the boat. Noah also had to bring every kind of animal and bird onto the boat with him and his family. God's commands about this boat and the creatures might have been strange to Noah, but he did things God's way. He and his family were the only ones saved in the massive flood. Noah knew that <u>choosing God's way was better than choosing his own way</u>.

Use the Clues!
(Bible Review)

Okay, let's see what you remember.

■ **How did Saul choose his own way over God's?** (by keeping some of the animals and taking the king captive in the battle, instead of killing every person and animal as God had told him)

■ **Why do you think Saul chose his own way?** (he wanted the things the Amalekites had, he didn't want to waste good stuff, he was greedy, he didn't think about the consequences of not following God's way)

■ **Why do you think Noah chose God's way instead of his own way?** (he believed God knew best, he had faith in God)

■ **What are some examples of how you might be tempted to choose your own way and not God's?**

Ask a volunteer to open the backpack and take out the map.

■ **How would a map be useful when you're hiking?** (shows you the way to go, keeps you from getting lost)

■ **How is this map a reminder that choosing God's way is better than choosing our own way?** (we know that God has a way for us to follow; just as a map shows the way to get somewhere, we can choose to follow God's way and know that we're making the best choice)

Hang the map on the tree branch or hiking bulletin board. Review the previous lessons by asking volunteers to explain what the other hanging items stand for. (See Resources for the meaning of the backpack items.)

BIBLE MEMORY WAYPOINT   Jeremiah 7:23
(Scripture Memory)

■ *Objective: Children will hide God's Word in their hearts for guidance, protection, and encouragement.*
■ *Materials: map puzzle pieces*

Read this week's memory verse from the craft paper. Point to each word as you read it:

Obey me, and I will be your God and you will be my people. Walk in all the ways I command you, that it may go well with you (Jeremiah 7:23).

After the children have rehearsed the verse several times, explain that 12 pieces of a map are hidden in the room. Let children work in pairs or individually to find a piece, then cooperatively assemble the map and read the verse. Pull random sections out, and have the kids repeat the verse for additional practice.

PRAYER STATION

- **Objective:** *Children will explore and practice prayer for themselves in small groups.*
- **Materials:** *copies of* StationMaster Card #5 *for each adult or teen helper*

Break into small groups of three to five children. Assign a teen or adult helper to each small group and give each helper a copy of *StationMaster Card #5* (see Resources) with ideas for group discussion and prayer.

SNACK STOP: WALKING STICKS (Optional)

If you plan to provide a snack, this is an ideal time to serve it.

- **Materials:** *large pretzel rods, chocolate syrup, caramel ice-cream topping, fruit-flavored syrup, apple butter, paper plates*

Distribute a pretzel rod to each child; make the syrups and toppings available so children can garnish their walking sticks. As they eat, discuss how to know if you're going God's way or your own way.

Note: Always be aware of children with food allergies and have another option on hand if necessary.

APPLICATION

- **Objective:** *Children will have opportunities to show how the lesson works in their own lives through activities and take-home papers.*

Some children's ministries may allow children to play outside at this point. If yours does not, choose one of the following activities.

Obstacle Course

■ *Materials: boxes, chairs, rope, hula hoop, buckets or small, clean trash cans*

Create an obstacle course in the play area using the items available. Make obstacles that children will slide under, crawl over, step in or through (hula hoop/buckets or trash cans), follow in a winding pattern (rope laid in zigzag pattern). Children can compete as teams or individuals.

 All Hands to the Wall

■ *Materials: paper cups or blocks*

Set up two lines of cups to start the wall. Give each child two cups. **Let's make a wall. Line up here** (point to spot). **When it's your turn, place your cups so they balance on the other cups in the wall.** Small classes will need students to take more turns to have a more substantial wall. Build as high and wide as possible.

You listened and built the wall the way I asked you to. You did it my way. When we listen to God and do things his way, we can accomplish great things. Lead class in applauding their efforts. If they want to, build another wall.

 ON THE FAST TRACK! *(Take-Home Papers)*

(Optional) Introduce the treasure box by asking: **Who would like to choose a prize from the treasure box?** Anticipate excited responses. Show *On the Fast Track!* take-home papers. **When you take this *On the Fast Track!* paper home each week and do the activities, your parents can sign the ticket that you finished the work. Bring the signed ticket back to choose a prize from the treasure box.** Distribute the take-home papers just before children leave.

LESSON SIX: Power Food

Feed on Power Food!

Memory Verse:
Jesus declared, "I am the bread of life. He who comes to me will never go hungry, and he who believes in me will never be thirsty" **(John 6:35).**
Note: Younger children may memorize the shorter version of this verse in bold print.

Bible Basis:
Luke 16:19–31; Mark 1:4–8

Bible Truth:
Our spirits need power food as much as our bodies do.

You Will Need:
- [ ] Trekking backpack
- [ ] Bible time dress-up box
- [ ] poster board
- [ ] magazines
- [ ] butcher paper
- [ ] paper bag
- [ ] jump rope or ball
- [ ] book (nature or animals)
- [ ] praise music CD
- [ ] healthy food (cheese stick, hard-boiled egg, etc.)
- [ ] package of dried fruit or fruit roll-up
- [ ] glue sticks
- [ ] *On the Fast Track! #6* take-home paper
- [ ] *StationMaster Card #6*
- [ ] *(Optional)* treasure box
- [ ] *(Optional)* snack: toothpicks, fruit cubes or slices (apple, orange, pineapple, kiwi, grapes)
- [ ] *(Optional)* Activity #1: lively praise CD, CD player
- [ ] *(Optional)* Activity #2: 1 set of Power Bar verses per student (see Resources pages 90–91), construction paper, stapler, markers, pencils, tape

When you see this icon, it means preparation will take more than five minutes.

GET SET!
(Lesson Preparation)

- Print today's Bible memory verse on poster board. Print the words with enough space to be cut apart: **Jesus declared, "I am the bread of life. He who comes to me will never go hungry, and he who believes in me will never be thirsty" (John 6:35).** Hang the poster on the wall.
- Photocopy *On the Fast Track! #6* for each child.
- Photocopy *StationMaster Card #6* for each helper.
- Have your two male actors for the Bible story time choose items from the Bible time dress-up box to highlight their characters.
- Place the jump rope/ball, book, praise music CD, and healthy food in the paper bag and set near the story area.
- Set out the Trekking backpack and *(optional)* treasure box.
- Mount a length of butcher paper on the wall at children's height, if using the Welcome Time Activity. Set the magazines, scissors, and glue sticks at tables nearby.
- Place the dried fruit in the backpack. Set the zipped-up backpack at the story area.
- Photocopy the Power Bar verses from Resources pages 90–91 (one set per child), if using Activity #2. Cut the bars along the dotted lines.
- Set up snack or outside play activities if you include these items in your children's ministry.

TICKETS PLEASE!
(Welcome and Bible Connection)

■ *Objective:* To excite children's interest and connect their own life experiences with the Bible Truth, children will make a collage and talk about what their bodies need to keep them healthy.

Welcome Time Activity: Healthy Body Collage

■ *Materials:* magazines, scissors, glue sticks, butcher paper or poster board

As children arrive, direct them to a table where the materials are laid out. Instruct the children to find pictures in the magazines of things their bodies need to keep them healthy. They'll cut them out and together make a collage. One child can make a title for the collage. As they work, ask the children why they're making the choices they are making and how the things they're choosing are healthy for their bodies.

Sharing Time and Bible Connection

■ *Materials:* paper bag, jump rope or ball, book (nature or animals), praise music CD, healthy food (cheese stick, hard-boiled egg, etc.)

Introduce today's lesson with an object lesson and discussion. As you talk, give every child the opportunity to say something. Ask a volunteer to take an item out of the bag without peeking. Have him or her give the item's name and what it's for. Ask successive volunteers to do the same with the remaining items.

■ **What do all these things have in common?** (they're all good for you; all help keep your body, mind, or spirit healthy)

■ **What kinds of things keep your body from being healthy?** (junk food, too many sweets, no exercise, too many video games, bad music, not enough sleep)

■ **What keeps your spirit healthy and strong?** (reading God's Word, memorizing Scripture, prayer, praising God, being part of a church fellowship, doing things God's way)

After this sharing time, help your students connect their discussion to the Bible story they are about to hear from Luke 16 and Mark 1.

Our bodies need power foods to keep healthy. Sugary things and chips taste good, but they don't give us energy or keep us healthy. Our spirits need power food too. Watching cartoons and reading comic books won't feed our spirits enough to be able to keep following God. So what are the spiritual power foods we need to be spiritually strong? Two people from the New Testament can help us understand.

ALL ABOARD FOR BIBLE TRUTH   Luke 16:19–31; Mark 1:4-8
(Bible Discover and Learn Time)

■ *Objective:* Children will study Luke 16 and Mark 1 and hear how a rich man had no spiritual health, but John the Baptist was wise about spiritual power food.
■ *Materials:* Trekking backpack with dried fruit or fruit roll-up inside

Today we have two guests. They're both actors pretending to be men who really did live back in Jesus' time. They're going to tell us their stories so we can see how <u>our spirits need power foods as much as our bodies do</u>. Choose two student narrators who will read portions of the Scripture passages to set the scenes. Ask one student to read Luke 16:19–22.

The rich man is with us today. He is not a happy guy. Tell us what happened to you after your wonderful life full of riches, buying anything you wanted, and eating all your favorite foods every day. Actor responds.

Why did you end up in hell, suffering forever, after your comfortable life on earth? Actor responds.

What understanding did you have about life on earth after you got to hell? Actor responds.

You asked that someone would talk to your brothers who were still alive. What did you want to tell them? Actor responds.

Thank this actor, who can leave. Step over to the other actor. Ask another student to read Mark 1:4–5.

Here's our second guest. What's your name? Actor responds.

Tell us why you were out in the wilderness, instead of working hard to have a life of enjoyment and buying the tastiest foods. Actor responds.

Why did you have such unusual clothes and eating habits? Actor responds.

You made some very different choices from our first guest. You lived in an unusual way. Tell us why. Actor responds. Thank actor, who then leaves.

Then summarize: **The rich man had a great life while he was living. He could buy what he wanted, including all the yummiest foods. He probably never felt hungry a day in his life. Do you think he thought about what his spirit needed to be healthy?** (probably not) **John knew that he needed food to stay alive, as well as spiritual food to be strong in following God. He ate some unusual things, but he was healthy. And most importantly, he knew God and kept his spirit healthy by getting to know Jesus more and more.**

Use the Clues!
(Bible Review)

Okay, let's see what you remember.

■ **What differences do you see between the two men in the Bible stories?** (the rich man had a nice life on earth, but he didn't feed his spirit and never knew God so he suffered in hell; John fed his body and his spirit with food that gave him spiritual power and a healthy body, he followed Jesus)

■ **Why didn't the rich man feed his spirit with good things from God?** (he thought he had everything he needed because he could buy so much, he trusted in his money instead of God)

■ **How did John show he was feeding his spirit and not just his body?** (he used his time and energy to do what God wanted, he would have talked to God and read Scripture to understand spiritual things)

■ **How should you and I feed our spirits power food?** (spend time talking to God, reading the Bible, listening in church, singing praise songs, thinking about what Jesus taught)

Ask a volunteer to open the backpack and take out the dried fruit.

■ **How would dried fruit be useful when you're hiking?** (gives you energy to keep going, feeds your body)

■ **How is this dried fruit a reminder that choosing God's way is better than choosing our own way?** (we can feed our spirits power food the same way we eat good food to give our bodies power and strength)

Hang the fruit on the tree branch or hiking bulletin board. Review the previous lessons by asking volunteers to explain what the other hanging items stand for. (See Resources for the meaning of the backpack items.)

BIBLE MEMORY WAYPOINT   John 6:35
(Scripture Memory)

■ *Objective: Children will hide God's Word in their hearts for guidance, protection, and encouragement.*

Read this week's memory verse from the poster. Point to each word as you read it:

Jesus declared, "I am the bread of life. He who comes to me will never go hungry, and he who believes in me will never be thirsty" (John 6:35).

After reading the verse from the poster a couple of times, use scissors to cut out one word or phrase, such as "bread of life." Hand the cutout part to a student. Have everyone say the verse again, stopping where the words are missing. The student holding the words says those, then the class resumes reciting the verse. Cut out another word or phrase. Continue this way until half the verse is missing, then see if anyone can say the verse from memory.

 ## PRAYER STATION

■ **Objective:** *Children will explore and practice prayer for themselves in small groups.*
■ **Materials:** *copies of* StationMaster Card #6 *for each adult or teen helper*

Break into small groups of three to five children. Assign a teen or adult helper to each small group, and give each helper a copy of *StationMaster Card #6* (see Resources) with ideas for group discussion and prayer.

 ## SNACK STOP: FRUIT KEBOBS (Optional)

If you plan to provide a snack, this is an ideal time to serve it.

■ **Materials:** *cubed or sliced fruit (apple, orange, pineapple, kiwi, grapes), toothpicks*

Let the children spear fruit pieces with toothpicks to make mini kebobs.

Note: Always be aware of children with food allergies and have another option on hand if necessary.

APPLICATION

- **Objective:** *Children will have opportunities to show how the lesson works in their own lives through activities and take-home papers.*

Some children's ministries may allow children to play outside at this point. If yours does not, choose one of the following activities.

 Freeze for All

- **Materials:** *lively praise CD, CD player*

Play the praise music as children hop, jump, and move in energetic ways around the room. Tell them when the music stops, they have to freeze in the exact position they're in. Stop the music at random times. Those who move during the silence (until the music starts again) sit out until the next round. Add interest to the game by calling out types of moves for the children to make: crab walking, doing leapfrog with a partner, duck walking, pretending to be a chicken, etc.

 Power Bars

- **Materials:** *Power Bar verses (1 set/student, see Resources pages 90–91), construction paper, stapler, markers, pencils, tape*

Students will create a "Power Bar." After choosing at least four verses from the 13 available, they will stack them and staple the packet of verses together on the left side like a booklet. Then students will wrap the packet with construction paper (like a candy bar wrapper) and tape it closed. They'll create a design on the Power Bar wrapper. They can name their Power Bar as they choose. Talk about how to get spiritual power during the week by reading the Bible, singing praise songs to God, and practicing memory verses.

 ON THE FAST TRACK! *(Take-Home Papers)*

(Optional) Introduce the treasure box by asking: **Who would like to choose a prize from the treasure box?** Anticipate excited responses. Show *On the Fast Track!* take-home papers. **When you take this *On the Fast Track!* paper home each week and do the activities, your parents can sign the ticket that you finished the work. Bring the signed ticket back to choose a prize from the treasure box.** Distribute the take-home papers just before children leave.

LESSON SEVEN: The Best in Hard Times

Memory Verse:
Come near to God and he will come near to you (James 4:8).

Bible Basis:
Judges 6:1–6, 11–16; 7:9, 19–23; Numbers 13:1–3, 17–33; 14:1–10, 26, 30

Bible Truth:
God has my best in mind, even when things are hard.

Trust God in Hard Times

You Will Need:

- [ ] Trekking backpack
- [ ] craft paper
- [ ] small balloons
- [ ] small bucket or garbage can
- [ ] waterproof matches
- [ ] Bibles
- [ ] pencils
- [ ] paper
- [ ] whiteboard
- [ ] *On the Fast Track! #7* take-home paper
- [ ] *StationMaster Card #7*
- [ ] *(Optional)* treasure box
- [ ] *(Optional)* snack: small, empty plastic jars with tight-fitting lids (1 per 2–3 students), clean marbles (2–3 per jar), cold, fresh cream, sliced bread, plastic knives, salt
- [ ] *(Optional)* Activity #2: cold play dough

When you see this icon, it means preparation will take more than five minutes.

GET SET!
(Lesson Preparation)

- ■ Print today's Bible memory verse on craft paper: **Come near to God and he will come near to you (James 4:8).** Hang the verse on the wall.
- ■ Photocopy *On the Fast Track! #7* for each child.
- ■ Photocopy *StationMaster Card #7* for each helper.
- ■ Set out the Trekking backpack and *(optional)* treasure box.
- ■ Chill play dough before class, if using Activity #2.
- ■ Place the waterproof matches in the backpack. Set the zipped-up backpack at the story area.
- ■ Set up snack or outside play activities if you include these items in your children's ministry.

TICKETS PLEASE!
(Welcome and Bible Connection)

- ■ **Objective:** *To excite children's interest and connect their own life experiences with the Bible Truth, children will try a difficult task.*

Welcome Time Activity: Tough Balloon Blow

■ *Materials: small balloons, small bucket or garbage can*

As children arrive, invite them to join a helper who is blowing up balloons. The object of this exercise is for children to attempt a difficult task. Have them try to blow up the balloons, then try to tie them closed. Helpers should assist only when children are becoming frustrated or exhausted. Once they have a tied, inflated balloon, they are to try to blow it into the can or bucket (make this part challenging, too). Talk about what kinds of things the children find difficult (a school subject, keeping their rooms clean, getting along with an unfriendly classmate, etc.).

Sharing Time and Bible Connection

Introduce today's lesson by discussing these questions with your students. As you talk, give every child the opportunity to say something.

■ **What is something you've had to do that you thought was pretty hard?**
■ **How do you feel about God when you're having a difficult time in life?**
■ **Why do you think God lets us go through hard times?** (to teach us something, to make us tougher, to give others a chance to help us, to show us how much he will help us)

After this sharing time, help your students connect their discussion to the Bible story they are about to hear from Judges 6 and Numbers 13.

It might not seem like it, but <u>God has our best in mind, even when something in our life is hard</u>. Jesus had some hard things in his life, and God knew it was only for the best. Of course, knowing that doesn't make the hard times go away. But it can make them easier to get through. Let's see how some people in the Bible experienced hard times and what God wanted for them.

 # ALL ABOARD FOR BIBLE TRUTH
(Bible Discover and Learn Time)

**Judges 6:1-6, 11-16; 7:9, 19-23;
Numbers 13:1-3, 17-33; 14:1-10, 26, 30**

■ *Objective: Children will study Judges 6 and 7 and Numbers 13 to discover experiences the Israelites had with two hard circumstances and what they learned about God.*
■ *Materials: Bibles, paper, pencils, whiteboard, Trekking backpack with waterproof matches*

Divide the class into three groups, with competent readers in each group. Assign one group the Judges passages, a second group Numbers 13:1–3 and 17–33, and the third group Numbers 14:1–10, 26, and 30. (The Numbers passage is divided between two groups because of its length.) Hand out Bibles. **Let's find out how <u>God has our best in mind, even when something in our life is hard</u>.**

Ask the children to read their passage as a group. Older children should help younger ones find the passage; all should follow along as one or more group members read it. After they've had time to read and understand what's going on, explain that the class is going to make a chart of the information.

Divide the whiteboard in half. On the left side, write "who," "their problem," "their actions," "the result." Start with the group who read the first segment of the Numbers passage; ask who the main people are and write the response opposite "who." Do this for "their problem," then ask the group who read the second part of Numbers the remaining two questions. Use succinct phrases in answers. Try to have all group members contribute to the discussion.

Next, ask the group with the Judges passage to contribute ideas for the same four questions, and write their input on the other half of the board.

These two stories tell us about two hard times the Israelites had. Which story shows us the people knew that God had their best in mind? (Gideon's) **Which story is an example of the people not believing God had their best in mind, even when things were hard?** (the story of the spies) **God never left the Israelites, even when they didn't believe he had their best in mind. But the people had harder times because they weren't trusting God during their difficulties.**

Use the Clues!
(Bible Review)

Okay, let's see what you remember.

- **What was the hard thing happening in the story about Gideon?** (the enemy Midianites were making life hard by taking the crops, animals, and homes of the Israelites)
- **What did God do for the Israelites?** (he gave them the victory over the enemy)
- **What was the hard thing for the Israelites when they were spying out Canaan?** (the spies said the people were strong and too many to conquer, their cities were hard to get into, and there were giants)
- **What did the Israelites miss because they didn't expect God had their best in mind?** (none of the Israelites—except two spies who trusted God—were able to live in the Promised Land)
- **What kinds of things can be God's best for us when we're going through a hard time?** (to learn to trust God no matter what, to learn to pray harder, to not give up, to end up with a better result that God had in mind but we couldn't see)
- **What do we do while we're in the hard time?** (be patient, let friends help us, not give up on God, praise God)

Ask a volunteer to open the backpack and take out the waterproof matches.

- **How would waterproof matches be useful when you're hiking?** (even if you get caught in the rain or fall into a creek, your matches will still work)
- **How are these matches a reminder that God has our best in mind, even when something in life is hard?** (even when we have problems and hard things happen, we can know God has our best in mind, the matches still work even after they've gotten wet and cold, and God still is working for us when we're having a hard time)

Hang the matches on the tree branch or hiking bulletin board. Review the previous lessons by asking volunteers to explain what the other hanging items stand for. (See Resources for the meaning of the backpack items.)

BIBLE MEMORY WAYPOINT
(Scripture Memory)

James 4:8

- *Objective: Children will hide God's Word in their hearts for guidance, protection, and encouragement.*

Read this week's memory verse from the craft paper. Point to each word as you read it:
Come near to God and he will come near to you (James 4:8).
To help children memorize the Bible verse, use these actions:
Divide the class into groups of two or four. Have the small groups face each other.
One (or a pair if a group of four) will whisper the first part of the verse to the others, and that child (children) will finish the verse in a whisper. Reverse the roles. Call out: **"Break!"**
The groups break up and re-form with others and repeat the verse in the same way.

PRAYER STATION

- **Objective:** *Children will explore and practice prayer for themselves in small groups.*
- **Materials:** *Copies of* StationMaster Card #7 *for each adult or teen helper*

Break into small groups of three to five children. Assign a teen or adult helper to each small group and give each helper a copy of *StationMaster Card #7* (see Resources) with ideas for group discussion and prayer.

SNACK STOP: BEATEN BUTTER (Optional)

If you plan to provide a snack, this is an ideal time to serve it.

- **Materials:** *clean, small plastic jars with tight lids (1 per 2–3 students); clean marbles (2–3 per jar); cold, fresh cream; sliced bread; plastic knives; salt*

Add cream to the empty jars until about one-third full. Add a couple of marbles. Tighten lids well. Have children take turns vigorously shaking the jars until butter is formed. Add a bit of salt to the fresh butter, and spread on bread for the snack. While shaking the jars, discuss how hard times are similar to what's happening to the cream in the jar. Getting shaken up isn't enjoyable, but the result is great. In the same way, God knows what will come of our hard times, as long as we keep trusting him and waiting for his best.

Note: Always be aware of children with food allergies and have another option on hand if necessary.

APPLICATION

- **Objective:** *Children will have opportunities to show how the lesson works in their own lives through activities and take-home papers.*

Some children's ministries may allow children to play outside at this point. If yours does not, choose one of the following activities.

Sharks and Minnows

Tell kids that some games are hard, but worth it if you keep playing. Choose two to four "sharks," and designate an area in the center of the play area where the sharks swim. Everyone else is a minnow and starts the game on one side of the play area. The goal is to "swim" back and forth across the play area, avoiding being tagged by a shark. Minnows who are tagged become seaweed and stand or kneel in the play area. They can't move around, but can tag minnows that come close to them. Play until only one minnow is left. Then play again with new sharks.

 Best Forms

■ *Materials: cold play dough*

Hand out the play dough and ask the children to squeeze and squish it in their hands. It's stiff at first, but as they press and work on it, it softens and can be shaped. Ask children to make their best replica of themselves. As they work, remind them that the play dough was easier to shape and form after it had been squeezed and pressed in their hands, like being shaped by God when we undergo hard times.

 ON THE FAST TRACK! *(Take-Home Papers)*

(Optional) Introduce the treasure box by asking: **Who would like to choose a prize from the treasure box?** Anticipate excited responses. Show *On the Fast Track!* take-home papers. **When you take this *On the Fast Track!* paper home each week and do the activities, your parents can sign the ticket that you finished the work. Bring the signed ticket back to choose a prize from the treasure box.** Distribute the take-home papers just before children leave.

Memory Verse:

A righteous man is cautious in friendship, but the way of the wicked leads them astray (Proverbs 12:26).

Bible Basis:

Acts 10;
Numbers 16:1–35

Bible Truth:

Choose friends who honor God.

You Will Need:

- [ ] Trekking backpack
- [ ] Bibles
- [ ] Bible-time dress-up box
- [ ] craft paper
- [ ] magazines
- [ ] goofy hat
- [ ] trendy purse
- [ ] cell phone
- [ ] old shirt
- [ ] rope
- [ ] glue sticks
- [ ] *On the Fast Track!* #8 take-home paper
- [ ] *StationMaster Card* #8
- [ ] (Optional) treasure box
- [ ] (Optional) snack: 10 ounces semi-sweet chocolate, 1/3 cup light corn syrup (for 4-5 children), wet wipes or damp towels, wax paper
- [ ] (Optional) Activity #1: rope (1 section per team)
- [ ] (Optional) Activity #2: clean, empty food cans and plastic bottles, google eyes, buttons, pipe cleaners, wire, yarn, felt, hot-glue gun, permanent markers, craft foam

GET SET!
(Lesson Preparation)

- 🕐 Print today's Bible memory verse on craft paper: **A righteous man is cautious in friendship, but the way of the wicked leads them astray (Proverbs 12:26).** Hang the verse on the wall.
- Photocopy *On the Fast Track!* #8 for each child.
- Photocopy *StationMaster Card* #8 for each helper.
- 🕐 Prepare the edible chocolate play dough if using the Snack Stop. Melt the chocolate in a microwave for 1 minute (stirring occasionally) or until smooth and creamy. Alternately, place the chocolate in a bowl over another bowl that contains hot, but not boiling, water. Once the chocolate has melted, add the corn syrup and blend. Pour the mixture onto a waxed paper sheet and spread the chocolate with your fingers until it's about 1/2 inch thick. Cover loosely with waxed paper and let it stiffen for at least a couple hours or overnight. The chocolate will become very pliable. Store in a plastic bag or container until class. Prepare as many batches as needed to serve your class.
- Set out the Trekking backpack and (optional) treasure box.
- Place the rope in the backpack. Set the zipped-up backpack at the story area.
- Set up snack or outside play activities if you include these items in your children's ministry.

When you see this icon, it means preparation will take more than five minutes.

 # TICKETS PLEASE!
(Welcome and Bible Connection)

■ **Objective:** *To excite children's interest and connect their own life experiences with the Bible Truth, children will create funny-looking people and talk about important qualities of a friend.*

Welcome Time Activity: Unique Buddies

■ **Materials:** *magazines, scissors, glue sticks, paper, markers*

As children arrive, direct them to the table where the materials are set out. A helper can be creating a funny image of a person as an example to the children. They will cut out different parts of people (legs from one photo, head from another, etc.) and assemble them in a novel way to create a one-of-a-kind person. They can draw in parts they can't find in the magazines. While working, engage the children in conversation about what qualities are important in a friend.

Sharing Time and Bible Connection

■ **Materials:** *goofy hat, trendy purse, cell phone, old shirt*

Introduce today's lesson with an object lesson and discussion. As you talk, give every child the opportunity to say something.

Ask for three volunteers. Place the goofy hat on one, give the trendy purse and cell phone to another (girl), and place the old shirt on the third.

■ **Which of these three people would you choose as a friend? Why?**
■ **What things should you think about when you choose friends?** (how much they want to follow Jesus, if they have things in common with you, what they believe, etc.)
■ **How much do you think a friend's beliefs could affect your beliefs about God?**

After this sharing time, help your students connect their discussion to the Bible story they are about to hear from Acts 10 and Numbers 16.

The people we spend time with make a difference in what we think and do. Friends who don't care about God or who go against what God tells us can keep us from following Jesus like we want to. That's why it really matters that we <u>choose friends who honor God</u>. Let's see how some people in the Bible chose friends.

ALL ABOARD FOR BIBLE TRUTH   Acts 10; Numbers 16:1–35
(Bible Discover and Learn Time)

- **Objective:** *Children will study Acts 10 and Numbers 16 and hear how Peter chose a friend, while Israelite malcontents got their friends in trouble.*
- **Materials:** *Bibles, Bible time dress-up box, Trekking backpack with rope*

Divide the class into two or four groups (depending on class size), with competent readers in each group. Assign each group one of the Bible texts: Acts 10 and Numbers 16:1–35. Hand out Bibles. **Let's find out why it's good to <u>choose friends who honor God</u>.**

Have children read their passage in their group. Older children will help younger ones find the passage; all should follow along as one or more group members read it. After they've read the passage, the groups will explain the main points of their passage using actors. One or more students will be narrators who read or describe from the Scripture passage, while the others choose clothes from the Bible time dress-up box and act out what is narrated. Helpers can assist the groups to summarize their stories for clarity.

After groups are finished, summarize the stories: **In Numbers, a man named Korah didn't like how Moses was the leader who got to talk to God and be in charge. Korah got all his friends to complain and rebel against Moses and Aaron, God's leaders of the people. Korah and his friends wouldn't listen to Moses, so God had to deal with them. God caused the earth to open up; Korah, his friends, and their families fell into the hole and died. Korah wasn't obedient to Moses, who was God's chosen leader. The people who chose to be Korah's friends died just as he did because they rebelled against God.**

In Acts, Peter was a Jew traveling around telling people about Jesus and salvation. Cornelius loved and served God, even though he wasn't a Jew. God gave Peter a dream that showed him he should be friends with Cornelius. This was weird for Peter because Jews didn't have friends who were not Jews. But when Peter saw that Cornelius honored God, he knew they could become friends.

Use the Clues!
(Bible Review)

Okay, let's see what you remember.

■ **Which story shows us that the friends who don't honor God are wrong for us?** (the story about Korah)

■ **Why was Korah not the kind of person to choose for a friend?** (he rebelled against Moses, who was God's leader)

■ **What did Peter learn about choosing friends?** (even someone who is from a different place and has different ways can be a friend if they honor God)

■ **Why does it matter whether or not our friends follow Jesus and honor God?** (if they don't they can cause us to walk away from God, the people we spend time with make an impression on us, people who are not God-honoring can cause us to not honor God also)

■ **How can you tell if someone is the right kind of friend?** (if they are walking with God and believe the Bible as you do, they can be a good friend)

Ask a volunteer to open the backpack and take out the rope.

■ **How could rope be useful when you're hiking?** (if you're trying to climb up a steep rock, or you fall and need to be pulled back up to the trail, a fellow hiker can use the rope)

■ **How is the rope a reminder to <u>choose friends who honor God</u>?** (someone who doesn't have the same values as you do might not be reliable to keep you walking with God, you want to be sure that the person trying to help you when you need to be rescued with the rope will save you, the wrong person on the other end of the rope could leave you in danger)

Hang the rope on the tree branch or hiking bulletin board. Review the previous lessons by asking volunteers to explain what the other hanging items stand for. (See Resources for the meaning of the backpack items.)

BIBLE MEMORY WAYPOINT
(Scripture Memory)

Proverbs 12:26

■ *Objective: Children will hide God's Word in their hearts for guidance, protection, and encouragement.*

Read this week's memory verse from the craft paper. Point to each word as you read it:

A righteous man is cautious in friendship, but the way of the wicked leads them astray (Proverbs 12:26).

Practice the verse by adding some fun actions. After saying it together a few times, ask children for actions that go with "listen," "accept," and "wise." You can break into small groups to practice with the actions, or do it all together.

PRAYER STATION

- *Objective: Children will explore and practice prayer for themselves in small groups.*
- *Materials: Copies of* StationMaster Card #8 *for each adult or teen helper*

Break into small groups of three to five children. Assign a teen or adult helper to each small group, and give each helper a copy of *StationMaster Card #8* (see Resources) with ideas for group discussion and prayer.

SNACK STOP: PLAY DOUGH ROPE (Optional)

If you plan to provide a snack, this is an ideal time to serve it.

- *Materials: prepared edible chocolate play dough, wax paper, wet wipes or wet cloths*

Hand out a portion of edible play dough. Ask children to shape a rope and talk about how friends can help each other. Children can sculpt other designs if they desire before eating their play dough.

Note: Always be aware of children with food allergies and have another option on hand if necessary.

APPLICATION

- *Objective: Children will have opportunities to show how the lesson works in their own lives through activities and take-home papers.*

Some children's ministries may allow children to play outside at this point. If yours does not, choose one of the following activities.

Rescue Relay

■ *Materials:* rope (1 section per team)

Divide into teams. Have each team choose a sound that will be their team call. After teams have chosen their call, have all the players, except those with the ropes, mingle in the play area. They must close their eyes and keep moving, walking, or shuffling so as not to injure others. The player with the rope "rescues" his team members by finding them according to the team call. Team members will make their sound while moving around waiting for rescue. When the rope carrier finds a team member, he places their hands on the rope. That player now holds onto the rope and follows the rope carrier as he searches for other team members. The first team to gather all their players on the rope wins.

Funny Friends

■ *Materials: clean, empty food cans and plastic bottles, google eyes, buttons, pipe cleaners, wire, yarn, felt, hot-glue gun, glue, permanent markers, craft foam, scissors*

Children can create a "friend" using a can or bottle as a body and adding body parts, facial features, and clothing as they choose. These funny friends can serve as reminders of the kind of friends they should be looking for. As they work, engage students in conversation about friends and friendship.

ON THE FAST TRACK! *(Take-Home Papers)*

(Optional) Introduce the treasure box by asking: **Who would like to choose a prize from the treasure box?** Anticipate excited responses. Show *On the Fast Track!* take-home papers. **When you take this *On the Fast Track!* paper home each week and do the activities, your parents can sign the ticket that you finished the work. Bring the signed ticket back to choose a prize from the treasure box.** Distribute the take-home papers just before children leave.

Be Content!

Memory Verse:

You have made known to me the path of life; **you will fill me with joy in your presence,** with eternal pleasures at your right hand **(Psalm 16:11).**

Note: Younger children may memorize the shorter version of this verse in bold print.

Bible Basis:

Matthew 20:1–15;
2 Corinthians 11:24–33; 12:8–10

Bible Truth:

Happiness is being content with the life God gives me.

You Will Need:

- ☐ Trekking backpack
- ☐ Bibles
- ☐ butcher paper
- ☐ markers or crayons
- ☐ pencils or fine-point markers
- ☐ craft paper
- ☐ bottle of water
- ☐ plate of goodies or cookies
- ☐ brown and tan construction paper
- ☐ *On the Fast Track! #9* take-home paper
- ☐ *StationMaster Card #9*
- ☐ *(Optional)* treasure box

- ☐ *(Optional)* snack: paper sack, individually wrapped snacks such as small cookies, dried fruit, cheese sticks, several crackers, trail mix (you can buy the snacks already wrapped or wrap them yourself with plastic wrap or zip-top bags)
- ☐ *(Optional)* Activity #1: dress-up clothes
- ☐ *(Optional)* Activity #2: removable round stickers (half to full sheet per student), fine-point markers or pencils

GET SET!
(Lesson Preparation)

- ■ ⌚ Print today's Bible memory verse on craft paper: **You have made known to me the path of life; you will fill me with joy in your presence, with eternal pleasures at your right hand (Psalm 16:11).** Hang the verse on the wall.
- ■ ⌚ Make a set of verse stepping stones for the memory verse practice. On sheets of brown and tan construction paper, write two or three words of the verse (including reference). Cut the edges of the papers to make them look like irregular stepping stones. Tape in a winding path.
- ■ Photocopy *On the Fast Track! #9* for each child.
- ■ Photocopy *StationMaster Card #9* for each helper.
- ■ Set out the Trekking backpack and *(optional)* treasure box.
- ■ Create a circle with tape or cones, if using Activity #1.
- ■ Place the water bottle in the backpack. Set the zipped-up backpack at the story area.
- ■ Set up snack or outside play activities if you include these items in your children's ministry.

When you see this icon, it means preparation will take more than five minutes.

TICKETS PLEASE!
(Welcome and Bible Connection)

■ **Objective:** *To excite children's interest and connect their own life experiences with the Bible Truth, children will decorate the classroom door to create a happy mood and talk about things that make them happy.*

Welcome Time Activity: Door Decor

■ **Materials:** *butcher paper, markers or crayons, tape*
As children arrive, direct them to the classroom door (or window) where you have taped the butcher paper. Tell the children their job is to decorate the door to give it a happy look. Encourage cooperative work as much as possible. Talk with the children about what kinds of things cause them to be happy and why.

Sharing Time and Bible Connection

Introduce today's lesson with an object lesson and discussion. As you talk, give every child the opportunity to say something. Show the children the plate of treats.

■ **Who would be happy to have this plate of goodies?** (expect a show of hands or verbal response) Take away half the goodies.
■ **Who would be happy with this plate of treats?** Allow responses.
Remove most of the remaining goodies.
■ **Who would be happy with this plate of treats?** Ask a child who responded positively why he or she would be happy with just a few treats.
■ **How much of something, like toys or clothes, do you need to be happy?** Allow responses.

After this sharing time, help your students connect their discussion to the Bible story they are about to hear from Matthew 20 and 2 Corinthians 11—12.
When we have lots of things, we might think it's impossible to be happy with less. But if you had nothing and then were given a small gift, do you think you would be happy with just that one thing? Television and other people try to show us what will make us happy. Today we're going to find out from some Bible people's lives that <u>happiness is being content with the life God gives us</u>.

ALL ABOARD FOR BIBLE TRUTH
(Bible Discover and Learn Time)

**Matthew 20:1–15;
2 Corinthians 11:24–33; 12:8–10**

■ *Objective: Children will study Matthew 20 and 2 Corinthians 11—12 to find out how Paul defined happiness and contentment, as opposed to some workers who worked different amounts of time for the same pay.*

■ *Materials: Bibles, Trekking backpack with bottle of water*

Divide the class into two or four groups (depending on class size), with competent readers in each group. Assign each group one of the Bible texts: Matthew 20:1–15 and 2 Corinthians 11:24–33; 12:8–10. Hand out Bibles. **Let's dig into the Bible to see how <u>happiness is being content with the life God gives us.</u>**

Have children read their passage in their group. Older children will help younger ones find the passage; all should follow along as one or more group members read it. After they've read the passage, the group should decide if their main characters were content with what they were given or not, and why or why not. Helpers can assist the groups to understand their stories if needed. When groups are finished, tell them you're going to ask them questions about their story. The people in each group should act as if they are the character(s) they read about and answer your questions the way those people would answer.

Start with the Matthew 20 passage:

Who were the main people in this story? (the landowner and the workers)

There were different groups of workers. Divide yourselves up to play the parts of the four groups. Wait as students do this, with helpers' assistance as needed.

Speak to the first group. **What did I, the landowner, do for you?** (hired them early in the morning for a set amount of money)

To second group, ask: **So what did I do for you?** (hired them at nine o'clock) Repeat for the remaining two groups.

Who got paid first? (the group that was hired last). Ask that group: **How much did you get paid?** (a day's pay)

Ask other groups: **What did you each get paid?** (the same as the group hired last) To the first hired group, ask: **How did you feel about how I paid all the workers?** (angry, cheated) What did the landowner tell the angry workers? (they got paid just what they had agreed on, it was the landowner's choice what to pay the workers, what's wrong with being generous) Thank the group(s), and turn to the 2 Corinthians group.

Who was the main person in your story? (Paul) **Pretend you're Paul. Tell what things happened to you?** Allow children to describe the trials Paul experienced. Try to have them share the telling, so all get to speak. **How do you feel about what's happened to you?** (he was content with weaknesses, insults, hardships, persecutions, and disasters for Jesus' sake) Thank the group.

Use the Clues!
(Bible Review)

Okay, let's see what you remember.

- **How happy were the workers who earned a day's pay for their work?** (the ones who worked all day were unhappy that others who worked less got the same pay)
- **What kind of attitude do you think would have been better, instead of being angry and jealous?** (happy that they got a job and got paid)
- **What did Paul have to be happy about, from his description in 2 Corinthians?** (nothing, except that he was still alive)
- **Why would Paul say he was content?** (God said he would give him strength when Paul was weak, knowing he could depend on God was enough for Paul to be content, he had learned to be happy with whatever God gave him)
- **In what areas can we begin to be happy with what God has given us?** (our families, our possessions, our friends, our health, our school situations)
- **How much do you need to be happy?** Accept reasonable responses.

Ask a volunteer to open the backpack and take out the water bottle.

- **How could a bottle of water be useful when you're hiking?** (you get thirsty, so it keeps you from becoming dehydrated)
- **How is the water a reminder to be happy with the life God gives me?** (compared to a bottle of sports drink or juice or soda, it might seem boring or plain, but it's all we need when we're thirsty; in the same way, if we have a place to sleep and clothes to wear and something to eat, we can be content; water reminds us to be content with what we have)

Hang the water bottle on the tree branch or hiking bulletin board. Review the previous lessons by asking volunteers to explain what the other hanging items stand for. (See Resources for the meaning of the backpack items.)

BIBLE MEMORY WAYPOINT
(Scripture Memory)

Psalm 16:11

- ***Objective:*** *Children will hide God's Word in their hearts for guidance, protection, and encouragement.*
- ***Materials:*** *Verse stepping stones*

Read this week's memory verse from the craft paper. Point to each word as you read it:

You have made known to me the path of life; you will fill me with joy in your presence, with eternal pleasures at your right hand (Psalm 16:11).

Lead the children along the winding verse path and read the steps as you go. Have pairs of children take turns hopping or walking along the path as everyone repeats the words.

 ## PRAYER STATION

- **Objective:** *Children will explore and practice prayer for themselves in small groups.*
- **Materials:** *Copies of* StationMaster Card #9 *for each adult or teen helper*

Break into small groups of three to five children. Assign a teen or adult helper to each small group, and give each helper a copy of *StationMaster Card #9* (see Resources) with ideas for group discussion and prayer.

SNACK STOP: SNACK SURPRISE (Optional)

If you plan to provide a snack, this is an ideal time to serve it.

- **Materials:** *paper sack with different, individually wrapped snacks*

Let children put a hand in the sack and pull out a snack. Children will have different types of snacks. Help them work on their responses, practicing to be happy with whatever they're given. Allow children to trade with one another at your discretion.

Note: Always be aware of children with food allergies and have another option on hand if necessary.

APPLICATION

- *Objective:* *Children will have opportunities to show how the lesson works in their own lives through activities and take-home papers.*

Some children's ministries may allow children to play outside at this point. If yours does not, choose one of the following activities.

Dress-Up Relay

- *Materials:* *dress-up clothes*

Divide into groups. Have groups choose a spot on the play circle, equally distant from other groups. Set some dress-up clothes near each group. One player at a time will put on one item and race around the circle. They'll keep the piece of clothing on during the rest of the game (unless clothing is limited and other players need it for their lap). After the game ends, ask children how they feel about what they're wearing. Remind them of the goal to be happy with what God gives them. Play again.

Happy Face Stickers

- *Materials:* *removable round stickers, fine-point markers or pencils*

Give each child a sheet of round stickers. Ask them to make happy faces on the stickers. They can be creative with their art. Talk about places they might put the stickers to remind themselves to be happy with whatever they have.

ON THE FAST TRACK! *(Take-Home Papers)*

(Optional) Introduce the treasure box by asking: **Who would like to choose a prize from the treasure box?** Anticipate excited responses. Show *On the Fast Track!* take-home papers. **When you take this *On the Fast Track!* paper home each week and do the activities, your parents can sign the ticket that you finished the work. Bring the signed ticket back to choose a prize from the treasure box.** Distribute the take-home papers just before children leave.

LESSON TEN: Under Authority

Under God Is Best!

Memory Verse:

Trust in the LORD with all your heart and lean not on your own understanding; in all your ways acknowledge him, and he will make your paths straight **(Proverbs 3:5–6).**
Note: Younger children may memorize the shorter version of this verse in bold print.

Bible Basis:

Numbers 12; Esther 2:15–20; 3:6–9; 4:7–14; 5:1–2; 8:1–8

Bible Truth:

The best place to be is under God's authority.

You Will Need:

- [ ] Trekking backpack
- [ ] Bibles
- [ ] craft paper
- [ ] blindfold
- [ ] people puppets
- [ ] whistle
- [ ] umbrellas (1 or more)
- [ ] *On the Fast Track! #10* take-home paper
- [ ] *StationMaster Card #10*
- [ ] (Optional) treasure box
- [ ] (Optional) snack: home-made or store-bought ginger or sugar cookies in people shapes, white frosting, plastic knives
- [ ] (Optional) Activity #1: 2–3 umbrellas
- [ ] (Optional) Activity #2: play dough or chenille stems

When you see this icon, it means preparation will take more than five minutes.

GET SET!
(Lesson Preparation)

- ■ Print today's Bible memory verse on craft paper: **Trust in the LORD with all your heart and lean not on your own understanding; in all your ways acknowledge him, and he will make your paths straight (Proverbs 3:5–6).** Hang the verse on the wall.
- ■ Photocopy *On the Fast Track! #10* for each child.
- ■ Photocopy *StationMaster Card #10* for each helper.
- ■ Set out the Trekking backpack and (optional) treasure box.
- ■ Place the whistle in the backpack. Set the zipped-up backpack at the story area.
- ■ Set up snack or outside play activities if you include these items in your children's ministry.

TICKETS PLEASE!
(Welcome and Bible Connection)

- ■ *Objective: To excite children's interest and connect their own life experiences with the Bible Truth, children will lead or follow in an obstacle course and talk about how they felt about not being in charge.*

Welcome Time Activity: Under Control Course

■ *Materials:* *blindfold*

As children arrive, ask the first ones to create a simple obstacle course using classroom equipment and furniture. Once chairs, tables, and trash cans are placed to navigate around, have children pair up. One will be blindfolded and under the authority of the partner who leads him through the course. After pairs have done the course once, they can change roles and do the course again. Ask them how they feel being in charge of the course versus being under the authority of their partner when blindfolded.

Sharing Time and Bible Connection

Introduce today's lesson by discussing these questions with your students. As you talk, give every child the opportunity to say something.

■ **What does it mean to be in authority over someone?** (to be in charge, to have control over what happens, to be responsible)
■ **How does it feel to be under another person's authority or control?** (safe, good, secure, frustrating, smothered)
■ **Who is in control or in authority over things you do?** (parents, teachers, coaches, older siblings)
■ **What would happen if you chose not to obey the authority over you?** (you get in trouble, could get hurt, have too much freedom, not know what to do, make mistakes)

After this sharing time, help your students connect their discussion to the Bible story they are about to hear from Numbers 12 and Esther.

God puts people over us as authorities to help us do what's right and to protect us. We show we agree with God's authority by having good attitudes and obeying those in control over us. If we decide we want to be in control of things when we shouldn't, we can get into sticky situations. Let's see how people in the Bible show us that <u>the best place to be is under God's authority</u>.

ALL ABOARD FOR BIBLE TRUTH
(Bible Discover and Learn Time)

Numbers 12; Esther 2:15–20;
3:6–9; 4:7–14; 5:1–2; 8:1–8

■ *Objective:* Children will study Numbers 12 and Esther and learn that Miriam and Aaron were unhappy with the authority God put over them, while Esther was willing to be under the authority of her uncle and the king.

■ *Materials:* Bibles, people puppets, Trekking backpack with whistle

Divide the class into two or four groups, with competent readers in each group. Assign each group one of the Bible texts: Numbers 12 and Esther 2:15–20; 3:6–9; 4:7–14; 5:1–2; 8:1–8. Hand out Bibles, paper, and pencils. **Let's find out why <u>the best place to be is under God's authority</u>.**

Have children read their passage in their group. Older children will help younger ones find the passage; all should follow along as one or more group members read it. Instruct groups to find out who is doing what in their passage. Make puppets available, and ask the groups to prepare a short puppet play about their Scripture passage. After a set amount of time, call the groups back together to present their plays. When all have performed, compliment their efforts.

Summarize the stories: **Moses was the leader God put in control of the Israelites. He had a big job, and the Israelites were safe and secure when they followed him. Miriam and Aaron were jealous because God talked to Moses but not to them. They weren't happy to be under his authority. They complained about him. God was angry at what they were doing. He called them outside their tent and scolded them. He punished them for not being happy under Moses' authority, and he made Miriam really sick. Moses asked God to forgive Miriam and show her mercy. After seven days, God made her well again.**

Queen Esther knew that she was under God's authority. She obeyed the king and her uncle Mordecai because they were the people God had put in authority over her. When her people, the Jews, were in danger, Esther didn't try to take control of the situation. She let God use her to save the Jews. Because Esther was happy to stay under God's authority, she was safe and so were all the Jews.

Use the Clues!
(Bible Review)

Okay, let's see what you remember.

■ **What did Aaron and Miriam do wrong?** (they complained about what Moses got to do as the leader, they showed they didn't like being under his authority)

■ **Why did God discipline them?** (they needed to accept the authority over them because God had put it there, they needed to accept that they weren't in control)

■ **Who was in authority over Esther?** (God, the king, Mordecai her uncle)

■ **How did Esther show she agreed with being under the control of those God had put in her life?** (she agreed to do as they asked, she showed her trust in them)

■ **Who might God put in authority over us?** (parents, teachers, grandparents, other adults, government leaders, law enforcement, babysitters)

Ask a volunteer to open the backpack and take out the whistle.

■ **How could a whistle be useful when you're hiking?** (if you get lost, you can whistle so others can find you)

■ **How is this whistle a reminder that the best place to be is under God's authority?** (a whistle can work for our good, just like the authority God puts over us, it can be used to call for order or help)

Hang the whistle on the tree branch or hiking bulletin board. Review the previous lessons by asking volunteers to explain what the other hanging items stand for. (See Resources for the meaning of the backpack items.)

BIBLE MEMORY WAYPOINT
(Scripture Memory)

Proverbs 3:5–6

■ *Objective: Children will hide God's Word in their hearts for guidance, protection, and encouragement.*
■ *Materials: 1 or more umbrellas*

Read this week's memory verse from the craft paper. Point to each word as you read it:

Trust in the LORD with all your heart and lean not on your own understanding; in all your ways acknowledge him, and he will make your paths straight (Proverbs 3:5–6).

Use the umbrellas to practice the verse. Depending on how many umbrellas you have and class size, use enough so that about a quarter to a third of the class can be under an umbrella at a time. Open the umbrellas (helpers or older children can hold them too).

Have the children mingle in the classroom. Those with umbrellas will walk among them, saying the verse in unison, and pausing randomly with the umbrellas over small groups of children. Whoever is under an umbrella says the verse with the umbrella holder until the umbrella moves again. Keep the umbrellas moving around the room with different batches of children saying the verse.

 ## PRAYER STATION

- **Objective:** *Children will explore and practice prayer for themselves in small groups.*
- **Materials:** *copies of* StationMaster Card #10 *for each adult or teen helper*

Break into small groups of three to five children. Assign a teen or adult helper to each small group and give each helper a copy of *StationMaster Card #10* (see Resources) with ideas for group discussion and prayer.

SNACK STOP: MIRIAM'S MISTAKE (Optional)

If you plan to provide a snack, this is an ideal time to serve it.

- **Materials:** *homemade or store-bought ginger or sugar cookies in people shapes, white frosting, plastic knives*

Give each child a cookie, and place the frosting containers and knives within reach. Have children retell the main points of the story of Miriam and Aaron. At the point where they tell of her getting leprosy because she rebelled against Moses' and God's authority, they can spread frosting on their cookies. As they eat, remind them that God took away the leprosy after seven days, when Aaron admitted they were wrong and asked forgiveness.

Note: Always be aware of children with food allergies and have another option on hand if necessary.

APPLICATION

■ *Objective: Children will have opportunities to show how the lesson works in their own lives through activities and take-home papers.*

Some children's ministries may allow children to play outside at this point. If yours does not, choose one of the following activities.

Umbrella Tag

■ *Materials: 2-3 umbrellas*

Play a version of tag using umbrellas. Designate one or more children as "It." Give helpers open umbrellas; they'll glide around the play area holding the umbrellas high above their heads. Those who take refuge under an umbrella are safe from being tagged. Limit how many can hide under an umbrella at a time. As the number of free players dwindles, remove one or more umbrellas. After the game, talk about how being under authority is a protection for us like umbrellas protect us from rain.

Follow the Leader

■ *Materials: play dough or chenille stems*

Hand out materials. Have a helper start by creating something simple with their play dough or chenille stem. Other children show they are yielding to the authority of the leader by following their example and making the same thing. Allow children to take turns being the leader and making something the others make in response. Discuss how giving up control to those in authority over you works out for the best and also pleases God very much.

ON THE FAST TRACK! *(Take-Home Papers)*

(Optional) Introduce the treasure box by asking: **Who would like to choose a prize from the treasure box?** Anticipate excited responses. Show *On the Fast Track!* take-home papers. **When you take this *On the Fast Track!* paper home each week and do the activities, your parents can sign the ticket that you finished the work. Bring the signed ticket back to choose a prize from the treasure box.** Distribute the take-home papers just before children leave.

LESSON ELEVEN: Hold It Lightly

Be Willing to Let Go!

Memory Verse:

Do not set your heart on what you will eat or drink; do not worry about it. But seek his kingdom, and these things will be given to you as well (Luke 12:29, 31).

Note: Younger children may memorize the shorter version of this verse in bold print.

Bible Basis:
Nehemiah 5:1–13;
Luke 12:22–34

Bible Truth:
Be willing to let go of whatever God has given you.

You Will Need:

- ☐ Trekking backpack
- ☐ Bibles
- ☐ play dough
- ☐ craft paper
- ☐ pretend money (from a board game or store, or homemade)
- ☐ wallet or purse or small bag
- ☐ strong suction cup
- ☐ blanket
- ☐ puppets
- ☐ *On the Fast Track! #11* take-home paper
- ☐ *StationMaster Card #11*
- ☐ *(Optional)* treasure box
- ☐ *(Optional)* snack: paper cups, sunflower seeds, chocolate-covered coins, plastic tablecloth
- ☐ *(Optional)* Activity #1: 3 colors of construction paper, sacks, boxes
- ☐ *(Optional)* Activity #2: shoeboxes or similar simple containers (baskets, sturdy bags, etc.), art supplies

When you see this icon, it means preparation will take more than five minutes.

 GET SET!
(Lesson Preparation)

- ■ Print today's Bible memory verse on craft paper: **Do not set your heart on what you will eat or drink; do not worry about it. But seek his kingdom, and these things will be given to you as well (Luke 12:29, 31).** Hang the verse on the wall.
- ■ If you don't have pretend money handy, make fake bills in denominations from $20 to $100, if using the Welcome Time Activity.
- ■ Photocopy *On the Fast Track! #11* for each child.
- ■ Photocopy *StationMaster Card #11* for each helper.
- ■ Set out the Trekking backpack and *(optional)* treasure box.
- ■ For each team in Activity #1, mix three colors of construction paper and place in a sack.
- ■ Place the blanket in the backpack. Set the zipped-up backpack at the story area.
- ■ Set up snack or outside play activities if you include these items in your children's ministry.

TICKETS PLEASE!
(Welcome and Bible Connection)

- ■ *Objective: To excite children's interest and connect their own life experiences with the Bible Truth, children will play a game about how they would spend fictional money and talk about their thoughts on money and possessions.*

Welcome Time Activity: More Stuff Charades

■ **Materials:** *pretend money, wallet or purse or small bag*

As children arrive, invite them to join a group playing a game of charades. Stash the play money in a wallet. A child draws out a piece of money and then acts out what he would do with that money if he really had it. Others try to guess what the person is acting out. After children have acted, talk about how people decide what to do with their money and possessions.

Sharing Time and Bible Connection

Introduce today's lesson with an object lesson and discussion. As you talk, give every child the opportunity to say something. Ask for three volunteers. Explain that you're doing an experiment. Attach the suction cup to the table or window. Once it's firmly attached, ask another child to try to take it off. Let volunteers try to remove the suction cup until one is successful (or they give up).

This suction cup really didn't want to let go of the table, did it? It's an example of how we hold onto things.

■ **Can you think of something you're attached to like this suction cup is attached to the table?** (pets, a certain toy, a piece of clothing, a photo of someone, etc.)
■ **What would cause you to give up some things that are important to you?** Allow for responses.

After this sharing time, help your students connect their discussion to the Bible story they are about to hear from Nehemiah 5 and Luke 12.

One thing we often forget is that everything we own comes from God. Once we get things, from toys and pets to money or clothes, we want to hold onto them and keep them for our own needs and desires. We have a hard time letting them go. We don't see how God may have a different use for our things. Instead of holding on tightly to things, we're wise to <u>be willing to let go of whatever God has given us</u>.

ALL ABOARD FOR BIBLE TRUTH   Nehemiah 5:1–13; Luke 12:22–34
(Bible Discover and Learn Time)

■ **Objective:** *Children will study Nehemiah 5 and Luke 12 to see what God wants us to do with the things he's given us.*
■ **Materials:** *Bibles, play dough, Trekking backpack with blanket*

Divide the class into two or four groups, with competent readers in each group. Assign each group one of the Bible texts: Nehemiah 5:1–13 and Luke 12:22–34. Hand out Bibles. **Let's find out the reason for <u>being willing to let go of whatever God has given us</u>.**

Have children read their passage in their group. Older children will help younger ones find the passage; all should follow along as one or more group members read it. Instruct groups to find out who is doing what in their passage. After the groups have read through the passage, give each child some play dough. Have group members work cooperatively to mold things that are mentioned in their text. After about five minutes, ask one or two group members to explain what their passage said, and let group members show what they shaped based on their reading.

Then summarize the stories: **Nehemiah was an Israelite leader who saw that some people with lots of money were taking advantage of those with less. They would lend money to people who needed it, then make them pay extra for it. If someone couldn't pay the money back right away, the wealthy people would take their things. Those who had little couldn't buy food or have a place to live. This was not the way God wanted people to use their possessions, and Nehemiah became angry with the wealthy people. He told them they needed to give back the things they had taken and be fair with the needy people.**

Jesus gave us examples of how to be willing to let go of the things we have. He said we don't need to worry about what we don't have because God will give it to us when we need it. He used flowers and birds to show us that they don't store up stuff as people do, because they let God take care of them. Jesus told us that instead of spending so much time thinking and taking care of things we own, we should put our time and what we have into things and people that will last forever—what God cares about most.

Use the Clues!
(Bible Review)

Okay, let's see what you remember.

■ **What problem did Nehemiah see among the Israelites?** (some were using their money and things to get more for themselves, they were taking advantage of others who had less, they were more concerned about their stuff and money than about what God cares about)

■ **What did Nehemiah tell them to do?** (to give back what they had unfairly taken and to be fair with others)

■ **What did Jesus teach about having stuff and money?** (to not be so concerned with what we have and what we want to get, to store up treasures in heaven, to be more concerned about what God thinks and wants to do with our things and money)

- **Why do things we own and our money matter to God?** (the way we use them shows what we think is important, we can use what he has given us for the things that last forever)
- **How much of our possessions and money are given to us by God?** (everything)
- **How tightly should we hold onto our things and money?** (very lightly)

Ask a volunteer to open the backpack and take out the blanket.

- **How could a blanket be useful when you're hiking?** (if the weather turns bad you could keep warm)
- **In case of cold weather, maybe hikers should take a windbreaker, a raincoat, a rain hat, and a portable heater. Would** just a blanket be enough? Accept responses, looking for an answer that God will provide what we need, instead of us trying to have everything that a hiker could possibly want.
- **How is this blanket a reminder to be willing to let go of whatever God has given us?** (remember that God provides what we need, so we don't have to hold onto all kinds of things and money, to hold lightly to things and trust God to give us what we need)

Lay the blanket under the tree branch or hiking bulletin board. Review the previous lessons by asking volunteers to explain what the other hanging items stand for (See Resources for the meaning of the backpack items.).

BIBLE MEMORY WAYPOINT
(Scripture Memory)

Luke 12:29, 31

- *Objective: Children will hide God's Word in their hearts for guidance, protection, and encouragement.*
- *Materials: puppets*

Read this week's memory verse from the paper. Point to each word as you read it:

Do not set your heart on what you will eat or drink; do not worry about it. But seek his kingdom, and these things will be given to you as well (Luke 12:29, 31).

To help children memorize the Bible verse, ask them to break out in small, mixed-age groups. Give an older child (or helper) in each group a puppet to use to coach the group as they learn the verse. After a couple of recitations, the puppeteer should pass the puppet on to another child. Once the verse has become familiar, say it together as a class.

PRAYER STATION

- **Objective:** *Children will explore and practice prayer for themselves in small groups.*
- **Materials:** *copies of* StationMaster Card #11 *for each adult or teen helper*

Break into small groups of three to five children. Assign a teen or adult helper to each small group, and give each helper a copy of *StationMaster Card #11* (see Resources) with ideas for group discussion and prayer.

SNACK STOP: SEEDS 'N' CHOCOLATE (Optional)

If you plan to provide a snack, this is an ideal time to serve it.

- **Materials:** *paper cups, sunflower seeds, chocolate-covered coins, plastic tablecloth*

Spread the tablecloth in the center of an open area. Have kids sit around the edge of the tablecloth. Pick one kid to sit in the middle and try to toss sunflower seeds into the other children's cups. Encourage children to use their cups to catch flying seeds. Pass out the chocolate-covered coins as well while you discuss how God provides.

Note: Always be aware of children with food allergies and have another option on hand if necessary.

APPLICATION

- **Objective:** *Children will have opportunities to show how the lesson works in their own lives through activities and take-home papers.*

Some children's ministries may allow children to play outside at this point. If yours does not, choose one of the following activities.

Hold It Lightly

■ *Materials: sacks with three colors of construction paper, boxes*

Today we found out that God wants us to be willing to let go of what he's given us. This game will help us remember to hold our things lightly.

Divide into teams. Set a box for each team at one end of the play area. Teams should space themselves, standing side to side, from their box to the opposite end of the room. At the end where they are stationed, set a paper sack filled with colored paper for each team. At "Go," the player of each team who's next to the full bag pulls out a sheet and passes it to the player in front of him, who continues passing it up the line. As soon as his hand is empty, the first player reaches for another piece of paper.

As the papers flow up the line, the players at the end drop them in the box. Intermittently, you will call out one of the paper colors. All players holding that color must drop that sheet immediately. Soon paper will be littering the floor. Keep calling out colors as the papers fly up the lines. After two to three minutes of play, call time. Helpers will count the number of sheets in the boxes. The team with the most in the box wins. Play again if time allows. Afterward, talk about how holding our things lightly, like the colored paper, means being ready to let go when we sense God prompting us to give away or use that thing for his purpose.

 "Hold It Lightly" Box

■ *Materials: shoeboxes or similar simple containers (baskets, sturdy bags, etc.), art supplies*

Distribute a box to each child to be decorated to his or her own liking. On the lid or in a prominent place, have the children write, "Hold It Lightly." Explain that this box will be a collection container for things they sense God is asking them to let go of. They might use it to put things they want to give to someone who needs it more than they do, or as a place to collect new things they plan to donate or share (school supplies, craft items, sports cards, pet goods). Or they could use it to collect things they need to get rid of because they have too many (extra hair accessories, excess fast-food prizes, etc.). Children might choose to use the box themselves or make it a family project.

 ON THE FAST TRACK! *(Take-Home Papers)*

(Optional) Introduce the treasure box by asking: **Who would like to choose a prize from the treasure box?** Anticipate excited responses. Show *On the Fast Track!* take-home papers. **When you take this *On the Fast Track!* paper home each week and do the activities, your parents can sign the ticket that you finished the work. Bring the signed ticket back to choose a prize from the treasure box.** Distribute the take-home papers just before children leave.

Memory Verse:

Great is the LORD and most worthy of praise; his greatness no one can fathom (Psalm 145:3).
Note: Younger children may memorize the shorter version of this verse in bold print.

Bible Basis:

Daniel 3:1, 8–26;
2 Corinthians 10:12–18

Bible Truth:

Praise God, not yourself.

You Will Need:

- [ ] Trekking backpack
- [ ] Bible time dress-up box
- [ ] Bibles
- [ ] craft paper
- [ ] flashlight
- [ ] CD player
- [ ] lively praise CD
- [ ] pretend microphones (paper towel tubes, large paper cups)
- [ ] *On the Fast Track! #12* take-home paper
- [ ] *StationMaster Card #12*
- [ ] *(Optional)* treasure box
- [ ] *(Optional)* snack: apple wedges, crackers, CD player, upbeat praise CD
- [ ] *(Optional)* Activity #1: flashlights
- [ ] *(Optional)* Activity #2: heavy cardstock, markers, glue sticks, rulers, praise words

When you see this icon, it means preparation will take more than five minutes.

GET SET!

(Lesson Preparation)

- ■ 🕐 Print today's Bible memory verse on craft paper: **Great is the LORD and most worthy of praise; his greatness no one can fathom (Psalm 145:3).** Hang the verse on the wall.
- ■ Photocopy *On the Fast Track! #12* for each child.
- ■ Photocopy *StationMaster Card #12* for each helper.
- ■ 🕐 If using Activity #2, cut heavy cardstock into long rectangles 12" long and about 2" wide. On the whiteboard, write praise words or use stickers with praise words for God's attributes and character.
- ■ Set out the Trekking backpack and *(optional)* treasure box.
- ■ Place the flashlight in the backpack. Set the zipped-up backpack at the story area.
- ■ Set up snack or outside play activities if you include these items in your children's ministry.

TICKETS PLEASE!

(Welcome and Bible Connection)

- ■ ***Objective:*** *To excite children's interest and connect their own life experiences with the Bible Truth, children will have fun praising God.*

Welcome Time Activity: Praise Karaoke

■ *Materials: CD player, lively praise CD, pretend microphones (paper towel tubes, large paper cups)*

As children arrive, invite them to join others doing karaoke to praise music. Let two to four students at a time sing or pretend to sing with the CD. Choose songs the children know. Those not singing can clap, tap their feet, and use their bodies in praiseworthy ways.

Sharing Time and Bible Connection

Introduce today's lesson by discussing these questions with your students. As you talk, give every child the opportunity to say something.

■ **Why do we sing praise songs like** _____ (name one or more used in the Welcome Time Activity, or that's familiar to children)**?** (to praise God, to worship God, to get our hearts in the right attitude for learning about him)

■ **How is praising God different from praising yourself?** (praising God is doing something God tells us to, praising ourselves is boasting or bragging or putting the spotlight on ourselves)

■ **What happens when a person gets used to praising himself instead of God?** (he thinks more of himself than he should, his eyes on are himself instead of God, he has a wrong picture of himself)

After this sharing time, help your students connect their discussion to the Bible story they are about to hear from Daniel 3 and 2 Corinthians 10.

It's not wrong to be proud of something you've done well. But when we start thinking we're pretty special or pretty smart or strong or anything else, we start to think of ourselves more highly than we do God. That's a dangerous thing! Let's see how some Bible people found out why it's smart to <u>praise God, not yourself</u>.

ALL ABOARD FOR BIBLE TRUTH
(Bible Discover and Learn Time)

**Daniel 3:1, 8–26;
2 Corinthians 10:12–18**

- ■ *Objective: Children will study Daniel 3 and 2 Corinthians 10 and understand how Nebuchadnezzar learned the hard way about praising himself, while Paul is a great example of boasting only in the Lord.*
- ■ *Materials: Bibles, Bible time dress-up box, Trekking backpack with flashlight*

Divide the class into four groups with competent readers in each group. Assign each group one set of verses: Daniel 3:1, 8–12; Daniel 3:13–15; Daniel 3:16–23; Daniel 3:24–26. Hand out Bibles. **Let's find out why we should <u>praise God, not ourselves</u>.**

Ask the children to read their passage as a group. Older children should help younger ones find the passage; all should follow along as one or more group members read it. Then children will quickly put together a simple drama to portray what is in their Scripture portion. Let children choose Bible time dress-up items (sharing among groups if necessary) and perform their drama in correct order.

You've read and seen how King Nebuchadnezzar wanted praise only for himself. He thought he was so important and powerful that he deserved everyone's praise. When three Jewish men wouldn't honor his statue, because they knew they could only show that kind of honor to God, he was really angry. Nebuchadnezzar was confused! But he found out that God honors those who praise him, and not themselves. The three men came out of the hot fire alive.

Paul was a man who spent many years serving God. He was a smart man who could have had lots of power and an important position. But he used a different measuring stick for himself. He said in 2 Corinthians that people who compare themselves with others so they can look good don't show good sense. Paul said the only thing he would boast or be proud of in himself was in sharing the news of 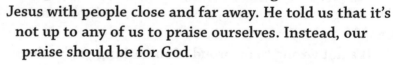 **Jesus with people close and far away. He told us that it's not up to any of us to praise ourselves. Instead, our praise should be for God.**

Use the Clues!
(Bible Review)

Okay, let's see what you remember.

- **What did Nebuchadnezzar want?** (he wanted everyone to honor the statue he made, he wanted everyone's praise for himself)
- **How did he find out that people should praise God, not themselves?** (God kept the three men safe when Nebuchadnezzar had them put in a burning furnace, he protected the people who praised him and not themselves)
- **What did Paul say about boasting?** (the only thing we should boast in is the Lord)
- **What did Paul say about comparing ourselves to others?** (comparing ourselves to others is using the wrong measuring stick, and it is not good sense, we should only boast in God)

Ask a volunteer to open the backpack and take out the flashlight.

- **Why might you take a flashlight when you're hiking?** (if it gets dark, you can find your way more easily)
- **How could this flashlight be a reminder to praise God and not ourselves?** (put the spotlight on God and who he is instead of trying to show off what you can do or be)

Hang the flashlight on the tree branch or hiking bulletin board. Review the previous lessons by asking volunteers to explain what the other hanging items stand for. (See Resources for the meaning of the backpack items.)

BIBLE MEMORY WAYPOINT
(Scripture Memory)

Psalm 145:3

- ***Objective:*** *Children will hide God's Word in their hearts for guidance, protection, and encouragement.*

Read this week's memory verse from the poster. Point to each word as you read it:

Great is the LORD and most worthy of praise; his greatness no one can fathom (Psalm 145:3).

To help the children memorize the verse, put the words to a rhythm and clap or stamp to the rhythm while chanting the words. Once you've practiced a couple of times, have the boys demonstrate, then the girls.

PRAYER STATION

- **Objective:** *Children will explore and practice prayer for themselves in small groups.*
- **Materials:** *copies of* StationMaster Card #12 *for each adult or teen helper*

Break into small groups of three to five children. Assign a teen or adult helper to each small group, and give each helper a copy of *StationMaster Card #12* (see Resources) with ideas for group discussion and prayer.

SNACK STOP: TOPPLING TOWERS (Optional)

If you plan to provide a snack, this is an ideal time to serve it.

- **Materials:** *apple wedges, crackers, CD player, upbeat praise CD*

Nebuchadnezzar built a statue that honored his power and greatness. We want to honor God's power and greatness. Challenge kids to build a tower of apple wedges and crackers. When it topples, tell them it reminds us that what humans can do is limited, but God's power and greatness are unlimited. While snacking, play the praise CD and encourage children to sing along.

Note: Always be aware of children with food allergies and have another option on hand if necessary.

APPLICATION

- **Objective:** *Children will have opportunities to show how the lesson works in their own lives through activities and take-home papers.*

Some children's ministries may allow children to play outside at this point. If yours does not, choose one of the following activities.

Flashlight Tag

■ *Materials: 1 or more flashlights*

This game requires a fairly dark play area. Give one or more helpers a flashlight. The children will try to stay out of the beam as those holding the flashlights shine them around the play area, trying to catch players in the beam. Any child caught in the beam goes to sit on the sidelines for the rest of the round. The last child playing wins. Before continuing for another round, ask: **Who should we spotlight with praise?** (God!)

 ## Measure of Praise

■ *Materials: heavy cardstock cut to size, markers, praise words, glue sticks, rulers*

Have children decorate a paper ruler that focuses praise on God. First they can draw inch or centimeter marks on their ruler, using a real ruler as a sample. Then they can draw, use stickers, or glue on praise words that focus on God's attributes and character.

 ## ON THE FAST TRACK! *(Take-Home Papers)*

(Optional) Introduce the treasure box by asking: **Who would like to choose a prize from the treasure box?** Anticipate excited responses. Show *On the Fast Track!* take-home papers. **When you take this *On the Fast Track!* paper home each week and do the activities, your parents can sign the ticket that you finished the work. Bring the signed ticket back to choose a prize from the treasure box.** Distribute the take-home papers just before children leave.

LESSON THIRTEEN: It's Not All about Me

Memory Verse:

For even the Son of Man did not come to be served, but to serve, and to give his life as a ransom for many **(Mark 10:45).**

Note: Younger children may memorize the shorter version of this verse in bold print.

Bible Basis:

Philippians 2:3–11; Matthew 23:1–11

Bible Truth:

Living for God is about serving, not being served.

Live for God!

You Will Need:

- [ ] Trekking back-pack
- [ ] Bibles
- [ ] cardstock
- [ ] glitter
- [ ] markers
- [ ] craft paper
- [ ] hiking boots
- [ ] shoe box
- [ ] colorful tissue paper
- [ ] various small items suitable for a care package
- [ ] *On the Fast Track! #13* take-home paper
- [ ] *StationMaster Card #13*
- [ ] *(Optional)* treasure box
- [ ] *(Optional)* snack: trays, cheese slices or cubes, crackers, napkins
- [ ] *(Optional)* Activity #1: small trays or plastic plates (1 per team), plastic containers and/or empty food containers (at least 10 per team—oatmeal or cereal boxes, plastic jars, empty soup cans), blocks or other toys, large boxes or bins (2 per team)
- [ ] *(Optional)* Activity #2: heavy paper towels or shop towels, crayons or colored pencils

 GET SET!
(Lesson Preparation)

- ◷ Print today's Bible memory verse on craft paper: **For even the Son of Man did not come to be served, but to serve, and to give his life as a ransom for many (Mark 10:45).** Hang the verse on the wall.
- Photocopy *On the Fast Track! #13* for each child.
- Photocopy *StationMaster Card #13* for each helper.
- Set out the Trekking backpack and *(optional)* treasure box.
- Make a tape starting line in the play area, if using Activity #1.
- Place the hiking boots in the backpack. Set the zipped-up backpack at the story area.
- Set up snack or outside play activities if you include these items in your children's ministry.

 TICKETS PLEASE!
(Welcome and Bible Connection)

- ***Objective:*** *To excite children's interest and connect their own life experiences with the Bible Truth, children will make a care package for someone.*

 When you see this icon, it means preparation will take more than five minutes.

Welcome Time Activity: Care Package Prep

■ **Materials:** *shoe box, cardstock, markers, glitter, colorful tissue paper, various small items suitable for a care package*

As children arrive, invite them to take part in helping assemble a care package for someone in the church (college student living away from home, military member overseas, person confined to home). Children can decorate the box, make cards to cheer the recipient, wrap the items, etc. Talk about how doing this project is serving someone.

Sharing Time and Bible Connection

Introduce today's lesson by discussing these questions with your students. As you talk, give every child the opportunity to say something.

I'm going to take a survey right now. I want to find out what you might want to be as a grown-up. Ask children to raise their hands if they want to be various types of workers (such as nurse, farmer, astronaut, pro athlete, chef, bus driver). After about six occupations, ask:

■ **Who would like to be a servant?** If anyone responds, ask why he or she would choose that role.
■ **What does it mean to serve someone?** (to do what they need to have done, to help them, to do jobs for someone)
■ **What is the life of a servant like?** Allow for responses.
■ **When was the last time someone served you?** Allow for responses.
■ **Why do you think many people wouldn't want to be a servant?** (it's hard, it's not fun, you aren't treated well, you can't choose what you want to do, people look down on you)

After this sharing time, help your students connect their discussion to the Bible story they are about to hear from Philippians 2 and Matthew 23.

Most people think that being a servant isn't a very good thing. It means doing what other people want and taking care of their needs. Servants aren't people you usually see in the news or who get awards or earn lots of money. So why would Jesus come to earth to be a servant? That's a strange idea—the Son of God coming here to serve people! Let's find out what Jesus says about <u>serving instead of expecting to be served</u>.

ALL ABOARD FOR BIBLE TRUTH   Philippians 2:3–11; Matthew 23:1–11
(Bible Discover and Learn Time)

- ◼ **Objective:** *Children will study Philippians 2 and Matthew 23 and compare Jesus' desire to serve with the Pharisees' attitude of superiority.*
- ◼ **Materials:** *Bibles, pencils, paper, Trekking backpack with hiking boots*

Divide the class into two or four groups with competent readers in each group. Assign each group one of the Bible passages: Philippians 2:3–11 or Matthew 23:1–11. Hand out Bibles, paper, and pencils. **Let's see the difference between <u>living for God as a servant compared to expecting to be served</u>.**

Ask the children to read their passage as a group. Older children should help younger ones find the passage; all should follow along as one or more group members read it. Once they've read through their passage, have them make a list of the attitudes and actions of the people or person being described. After the lists are compiled, ask the groups to share what they found.

Summarize the two stories: **In Matthew, Jesus was speaking to a crowd of people. He was describing a group of religious leaders who thought they should be served. These people would expect others to do the things they taught, but they wouldn't do these things themselves. The Pharisees did their actions just to look important to others. They loved to sit in the seats of honor at banquets and take the best seats in the synagogues, which are the Jewish places of worship. These religious leaders wanted everyone to notice them and call them "rabbi," which was an honored title. But Jesus said these people were doing everything against God's ways. God teaches us to be humble and to serve others.**

In Philippians, we have a description of Jesus. He showed us that our reason for doing something wasn't to make life easier or better for ourselves. Instead, we should be caring more about helping others. Jesus said not to be concerned about your own problems and needs, but to look out for the concerns of others. Jesus is described in these verses as being totally willing to serve people, even in dying. He didn't try to look important because he was God's Son. He actually did the work of a servant while he was here, as an example to us of how we should live to serve others, and not expect to be served ourselves.

Use the Clues!
(Bible Review)

Okay, let's see what you remember.

■ **Since the Pharisees were religious leaders, why were they wrong in their attitudes and actions?** (they expected everyone to treat them special and serve them, and didn't have any desire to serve others)

■ **Why were they wrong to want the best of things for themselves?** (because they had no concern for the needs of others they didn't follow Jesus' example of serving; they thought they were better than others, which Jesus said was totally wrong)

■ **How did Jesus show us to live?** (to be more concerned with the needs of others than of ourselves, to not think that our title or position in life gives us special privileges, that being humble as a servant is the best and right thing to be)

■ **How did Jesus serve while he was on earth?** (he fed people, he made sick people well and brought dead people back to life, he helped fishermen find fish, and most of all he died in our place)

■ **How can you and I live like Jesus says and serve others instead of expecting to be served?** (stop being so wrapped up in our own needs and wants, look for ways to help and take care of those around us, stop putting ourselves first)

Ask a volunteer to open the backpack and take out the hiking boots.

■ **How would these boots be useful for hiking?** (you can go farther in boots than softer shoes and not be worried about the rugged ground, your feet will be protected)

■ **How could these hiking boots be a reminder that living for God is about serving, not being served?** (wearing hiking boots gives you the ability to hike where other people might not be able to go, when you put on hiking boots you know what you're going to be doing, a servant may not dress in a certain way, but in his mind and heart he knows what he's going to do—serve others and not wait for others to serve him)

Lay the boots at the base of the tree branch or hiking bulletin board. Review the previous lessons by asking volunteers to explain what the other items stand for. (See Resources for the meaning of the backpack items.)

BIBLE MEMORY WAYPOINT
(Scripture Memory)

Mark 10:45

■ *Objective: Children will hide God's Word in their hearts for guidance, protection, and encouragement.*

Read this week's memory verse from the paper. Point to each word as you read it:

For even the Son of Man did not come to be served, but to serve, and to give his life as a ransom for many (Mark 10:45).

To help the children memorize the verse, practice it as an echo. Divide into two groups and have the groups face each other. One group says a phrase and the other group echoes it. Continue until the verse is done. Encourage the group starting the echo to use different kinds of voices (high-pitched, soft, singsong, rap style, etc.).

PRAYER STATION

- **Objective:** *Children will explore and practice prayer for themselves in small groups.*
- **Materials:** *copies of* StationMaster Card #13 *for each adult or teen helper*

Break into small groups of three to five children. Assign a teen or adult helper to each small group, and give each helper a copy of *StationMaster Card #13* (see Resources) with ideas for group discussion and prayer.

SNACK STOP: SNACK À LA SERVANT (Optional)

If you plan to provide a snack, this is an ideal time to serve it.

- **Materials:** *trays, cheese slices or cubes, crackers, napkins*

Let the children practice serving. Some can portion out cheese and crackers on napkins. Others can place the portions on trays. Several can carry the trays around to serve, and others can do cleanup.

Note: Always be aware of children with food allergies and have another option on hand if necessary.

APPLICATION

■ **Objective:** *Children will have opportunities to show how the lesson works in their own lives through activities and take-home papers.*

Some children's ministries may allow children to play outside at this point. If yours does not, choose one of the following activities.

 ## Serving Relay

■ **Materials:** *small trays or plastic plates, lots of plastic containers and/or empty food containers (at least 10 items per team), large boxes or bins, blocks or other toys*

Divide the class into teams who line up behind a tape line. At the opposite side of the room, designate a box or bin for each team. Place an equal amount of items in each team's box. Place an empty box or bin behind each team's line.

Hand the first person in each team a tray. Team members will take turns running to the full box, loading up their tray, and racing back to their team with the loaded tray to dump the items into the empty box. Anything that falls must go back to the original box to be carried by a later player. Continue until all the items have been successfully transferred.

 ## Server's Towel

■ **Materials:** *heavy paper towels or shop towels, crayons or colored pencils*

Children will make a server's towel, which they can drape over a forearm to portray a waiter in a formal restaurant. Demonstrate how to carry the towel, and explain that waiters used to carry them to wipe up spills and dry off wet bottles of beverages before serving them to diners. Children will draw or write the kinds of things they can do to serve in the places they spend their time (home, school, church, baby-sitters, etc.). Encourage creativity and practicality. Ask them to bring back reports next week of how their serving went.

 ## ON THE FAST TRACK! *(Take-Home Papers)*

(Optional) Introduce the treasure box by asking: **Who would like to choose a prize from the treasure box?** Anticipate excited responses. Show *On the Fast Track!* take-home papers. **When you take this *On the Fast Track!* paper home each week and do the activities, your parents can sign the ticket that you finished the work. Bring the signed ticket back to choose a prize from the treasure box.** Distribute the take-home papers just before children leave.

Room set up

Plant a sturdy tree branch in a bucket of dirt or sand and place near your story area. You'll hang the weekly reminders of the lessons on this or place them at the base and use the items during the review time. Alternately, decorate a bulletin board near the story area in a hiking theme and hang the items on the bulletin board.

1. **Trail mix:** God gives us things so we can be generous with others.

2. **Mirror:** What God thinks of us is the most important. Remember what God sees when he looks at us, and not what other people see.

3. **Compass:** Points to the right direction, like godly wisdom helps us be right, instead of trying to be right on our own.

4. **Binoculars:** Like binoculars bring faraway things into view, God's justice brings fairness into clear view.

5. **Map:** We know that God has a way for us to follow; we can choose to follow God's way.

6. **Fruit:** We should feed our spirits power food the same way we eat good food to give our bodies power and strength.

7. **Waterproof matches:** The matches still work even after they've gotten wet and cold, and God still is working for us when we're having a hard time.

8. **Rope:** Someone who doesn't have the same values as you might not be reliable to keep you walking with God. You want to be sure that the person trying to help you when you need to be rescued with the rope will save you.

9. **Bottle of water:** It's all we need when we're thirsty. In the same way, if we have a place to sleep and clothes to wear and something to eat, we can be content. Water reminds us to be content with what we have.

10. **Whistle:** Instead of feeling like we should be in control and have all the answers, we can be glad to have others in authority over us, because God put them there for our good. A whistle can work for our good, just like authority over us.

11. **Blanket:** God will provide what we need, instead of us trying to have everything that a hiker could possibly want.

12. **Flashlight:** Put the spotlight on God and who he is instead of trying to show off what you can do or be.

13. **Hiking boots:** When you put on hiking boots, you know what you're going to be doing. A servant may not dress in a certain way, but in his mind and heart, he knows what he's going to do—serve others and not wait for others to serve him.

Message Strips—*For use with Lesson 2*

God thinks **YOU'RE COOL.**

You're **SPECIAL.**

God **LOVES** you.

No one could love you **MORE THAN GOD.**

Nothing is more **IMPORTANT** to God than **YOU.**

God holds **YOU** close to his **HEART.**

God thinks **YOU'RE COOL.**

You're **SPECIAL.**

God **LOVES** you.

No one could love you **MORE THAN GOD.**

Nothing is more **IMPORTANT** to God than **YOU.**

God holds **YOU** close to his **HEART.**

Who's Right?—*For use with Lesson 3*

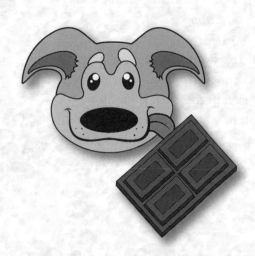

TRUE or FALSE?

Eating chocolate can kill dogs.

Answer: True, the most dangerous kinds are
unsweetened baking chocolate and powdered cocoa.

TRUE or FALSE?

Elephants are afraid of mice.

Answer: False. Actually, most elephants
don't show much fear at all.

TRUE or FALSE?

Throwing rice at weddings
is a bad idea because birds
eating it can explode.

Answer: False. It is actually an important
part of some birds' diets.

TRUE or FALSE?

The combined weight of all the ants
on earth equals that of humans.

Answer: True. They are tiny, but because of their
amazing numbers, they do weigh the same.

TRUE or FALSE?

Some red food coloring is made from ground-up beetles.

Answer: True. Many fruit juices, candies, and gelatin contain pigments that come from the shell of a beetle found in South and Central America.

TRUE or FALSE?

If you crack your knuckles, they will get bigger.

Answer: False. The sound is just the release of gases from the joint.

TRUE or FALSE?

If you swallow gum, it will take seven years to pass through your system.

Answer: False. It is not digestible, but will pass through like everything else.

TRUE or FALSE?

If you cover a wart with duct tape, it will go away.

Answer: True. This actually works better than freezing it.

Advice Letter—*For use with Lesson 3*

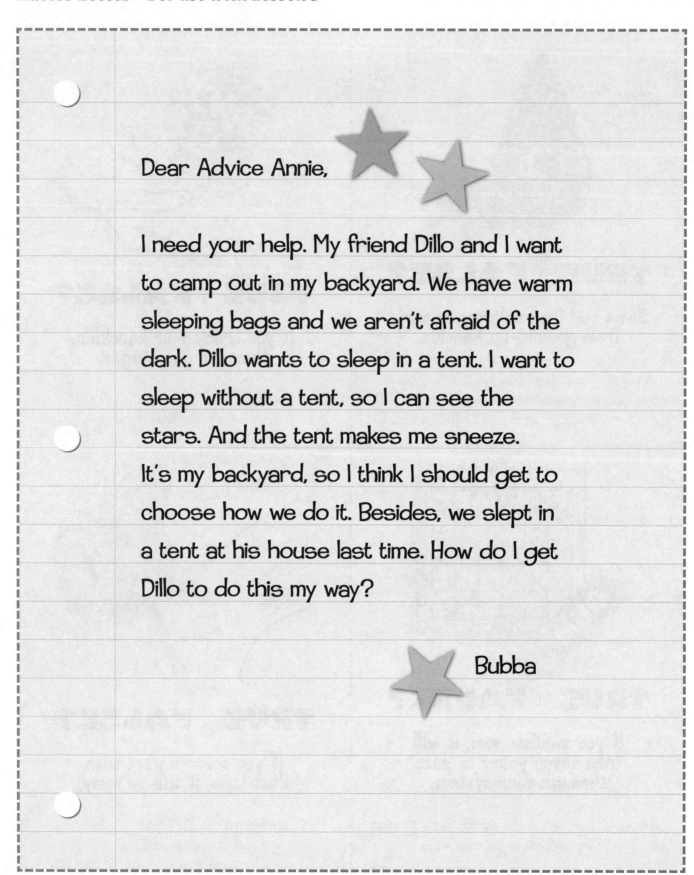

Dear Advice Annie,

I need your help. My friend Dillo and I want to camp out in my backyard. We have warm sleeping bags and we aren't afraid of the dark. Dillo wants to sleep in a tent. I want to sleep without a tent, so I can see the stars. And the tent makes me sneeze. It's my backyard, so I think I should get to choose how we do it. Besides, we slept in a tent at his house last time. How do I get Dillo to do this my way?

Bubba

Fair/Unfair Situation Cards—*For use with Lesson 4*

◎ **You did a lot of work on a school project, but your classmate took the credit for it.** *(unfair)*

◎ **You did a lot of work on a school project and the teacher gave you an "A."** *(fair)*

◎ **You and your sister were playing, and she screamed. Your mother came out, saw you were playing, and left you to continue.** *(fair)*

◎ **You and your sister were playing, and she screamed. Your mother thought that you hurt her because you were fighting, and you got in trouble.** *(unfair)*

◎ **Everybody else got the piece of candy they wanted. By the time it was your turn, all the good candy was gone.** *(unfair)*

◎ **Everybody was able to choose the piece of candy that they wanted.** *(fair)*

Power Bar Verses—*For use with Lesson 6*

LESSON 1:
A generous man will prosper; he who refreshes others will himself be refreshed (Proverbs 11:25).

LESSON 4:
Blessed are they who maintain justice, who constantly do what is right (Psalm 106:3).

LESSON 2:
Humble yourselves before the Lord, and he will lift you up (James 4:10).

LESSON 5:
Do nothing out of selfish ambition or vain conceit, but in humility consider others better than yourselves. Each of you should look not only to your own interests, but also to the interests of others (Philippians 2:3-4).

LESSON 3:
The fear of the LORD is the beginning of wisdom; all who follow his precepts have good understanding (Psalm 111:10).

LESSON 6:
Jesus declared, "I am the bread of life. He who comes to me will never go hungry, and he who believes in me will never be thirsty" (John 6:35).

LESSON 7:
Come near to God
and he will come near to you
(James 4:8).

LESSON 10:
Trust in the LORD with all your heart
and lean not on your own understanding;
in all your ways acknowledge him,
and he will make your paths straight
(Proverbs 3:5-6).

LESSON 8:
Listen to advice and
accept instruction, and in
the end you will be wise
(Proverbs 19:20).

LESSON 11:
Do not set your heart on what you
will eat or drink; do not worry about
it. But seek his kingdom, and these
things will be given to you as well
(Luke 12:29, 31).

LESSON 9:
You have made known to me the
path of life; you will fill me with
joy in your presence, with eternal
pleasures at your right hand
(Psalm 16:11).

LESSON 12:
Great is the LORD
and most worthy of praise;
his greatness no one can fathom
(Psalm 145:3).

LESSON 13:
For even the Son of Man did not
come to be served, but to serve,
and to give his life as a ransom
for many (Mark 10:45).

Dear Parents,

During the next 13 weeks in children's ministry, your child will learn about choosing to walk God's path rather than going the way of the world. Our *Stepping Up/Stepping Out* curriculum helps kids learn to make good choices in an exciting and interactive way and gives children an opportunity to build lifetime habits of choosing God's way. Each week, your children will get to choose whether their way or God's way will equip them better and how to compare good choices with things that will slow them down on their path.

Stepping Up/Stepping Out uses the **imPACT** model of prayer to help children understand the four important activities of prayer—praise, ask, confess, and thanks. Here are some discussion questions you may use at home to reinforce your child's growing desire to talk with God:

■ *Praise.* Ask your child: **What do you really like about God?** Listen to the responses. Then say: **Let's tell God we like these things about him.** Encourage your child to tell God directly what he or she likes about him.

■ *Ask.* It is important for children to know that God cares about their needs. We can ask God to help us, our families, and our friends with any problems. He wants everyone to ask him for what they need. Ask: **What would you like to ask God?** Let your child name some prayer requests. Then say: **Let's tell God about these needs.** Take turns praying for these needs.

■ *Confess.* Tell your child that we all do things we wish we didn't do. Sometimes our actions or words hurt someone and then we are sorry. Ask: **What's one thing that you wish you didn't do this last week?** Listen to the response. Then say: **Let's confess our sin to God and tell him we're sorry.** Together, bow heads and confess this sin before God.

■ *Thanks.* Ask: **What are some things that you're thankful that God has done for you or has given to you?** Listen to the responses. Then say: **Let's tell God thank you for these things.** Take turns thanking God.

Since prayer is such an important concept, your child will receive a take-home paper for each lesson, designed to support the Bible Truth for that day. These take-home papers will include fun activities, a Bible memory verse, and a prayer challenge. Some of the activities invite the involvement of the whole family. Encourage your child to complete these activities and bring the signed *Fast Track!* ticket the following Sunday.

If you have any questions about this study, please feel free to discuss them with the children's ministry leaders. We are excited about what God is going to do in the lives of our children. We would appreciate your prayers for the teachers and children.

In His Name,

Children's Ministry Coordinator

Dear Children's Ministry Helper,

Welcome to *Discipleship Junction*! During the next 13 weeks, you will play a major role in the lives of children as you teach them about making good choices and pray with them in small groups.

The *Stepping Up/Stepping Out* curriculum will help your kids build habits of choosing to go God's way rather than believing the world's message. You will reinforce these lessons even as you help build habits of prayer into their lives in a way that will last a lifetime.

The **imPACT** model of prayer will remind children about the four important activities of prayer: praise, ask, confess, and thanks:

■ *Praise.* Ask: **What do you really like about God?** Let volunteers briefly respond, then say: **Let's tell God we like these things about him.** Help children talk to God directly.

■ *Ask.* Ask children: **What would you like to ask God?** Allow children to give prayer requests, then say: **Let's tell God about these needs.** It is important for children to know that God cares about everyone's needs. Have them take turns praying for the needs in their lives.

■ *Confess.* We all do things we wish we didn't do. Sometimes our actions or words hurt someone and then we are sorry. Ask them: **What's one thing that you wish you didn't do this last week?** Give children time to answer, then say: **Let's confess our sins to God and tell him we're sorry.**

■ *Thanks.* When giving thanks, ask your group: **Tell one thing that you're thankful that God has done for you.** Let children share, then say: **Let's tell God thank you for these things.**

The children's ministry appreciates the important role that you have volunteered to fill. We are confident that God is going to do amazing things in the lives of our children.

Sincerely,

Children's Ministry Coordinator

StationMaster Card #1

This week your group learned from Genesis 13 and Matthew 19 that *God gives me things so I can be generous with others.* Lead your group in prayer in the following way.

■ *Praise.* **God is generous to us.** Encourage students to offer praise to God for the array of things he has given them, from people to things to places they love.

■ *Ask.* **How can you be generous with the things God has given you?** Give students the opportunity to ask God to show them specific ways to share their things.

■ *Confess.* **Many times we want something more than we want God.** Lead the students in confessing their greed or selfishness and asking his forgiveness.

■ *Thank.* **God is so generous to us and provides us with a lot of stuff.** Have students thank God for intangibles, such as nature's beauty, friendships, family love, etc.

Remember that no child should be forced to pray, but do encourage and invite each one. After you've said, "Amen," talk quietly with the children until the next activity.

StationMaster Card #2

This week your group learned from Daniel 1 and Acts 4—5 that *what God thinks of me is more important than what others think.* Lead your group in prayer in the following way.

- *Praise.* **God knows everything about us, and he thinks we're special with our differences and unusual features.** Have students praise God for knowing them completely, making them wonderfully, and loving them totally.
- *Ask.* **When we can't tell what is best to do, we should ask God. He's ready to point us in the right direction.** Give students opportunity to ask God for wisdom and direction in doing what he thinks is best in specific instances they are concerned about.

- *Confess.* **Sometimes we want other people to think we're pretty tough or smart or cool. We forget that what God thinks is the most important.** Model for students a prayer of confession, asking forgiveness for being more concerned with others' opinions than his.
- *Thank.* **God wants the very best for us and knows how to help us get it.** Lead students in sentence prayers of thanksgiving for how he is always seeking our best and leading us on his path.

Remember that no child should be forced to pray, but do encourage and invite each one. After you've said, "Amen," talk quietly with the children until the next activity.

StationMaster Card #3

This week your group learned from Genesis 4 and 2 Chronicles 1 that *having godly wisdom is better than being right all the time.* Lead your group in prayer in the following way.

- *Praise.* **God is perfect, which means that he is always right.** Lead students in praising God for being right and knowing what's best in every situation.
- *Ask.* **We always need help from God to know what is right.** Have students ask God for his wisdom in specific situations in their lives.
- *Confess.* **Sometimes we don't want to admit we're wrong or that someone else has a**

better idea. Give students time to silently or publicly ask God for forgiveness for a time they've insisted they were right and didn't care what others thought or felt.
- *Thank.* **God loves to give us wisdom and a new chance to learn to use it. Let's tell God "thank you" for giving us wisdom and helping us learn not to insist on having our own way.**

Remember that no child should be forced to pray, but do encourage and invite each one. After you've said, "Amen," talk quietly with the children until the next activity.

StationMaster Card #4

This week your group learned from 1 Samuel 2 and 1 Kings 3 that *God's justice shows me what is fair.* Lead your group in prayer in the following way.

- *Praise.* **God is always fair and just.** Have students praise God for his justice.
- *Ask.* **Are there some situations where you feel you haven't been treated fairly? Right now you can talk to God about that and ask him to cause his justice to show up in that situation.**
- *Confess.* **Sometimes we're more concerned about having our own way instead of being fair.** Give students time to listen to the Holy Spirit prompting them to confess sin and receive forgiveness.

- *Thank.* **It was unfair to Jesus for him to die for our sins.** Have students thank Jesus for his willingness to die for our sins so that we can spend eternity with him.

*** *If there are any children in your group who have not heard what Jesus did for them, or if they have never accepted him as Savior, this would be a good time to talk with them about it.*

Remember that no child should be forced to pray, but do encourage and invite each one. After you've said, "Amen," talk quietly with the children until the next activity.

StationMaster Card #5

This week children heard from 1 Samuel 15 and Genesis 6—7 that *choosing God's way is better than choosing their way.* Lead your group in prayer in the following way.

- *Praise.* **God is able to see how things will work out for us.** Lead students in praising God for his awesome abilities: knowing everything, having our best in mind all the time, and knowing the way we should go.
- *Ask.* **Deciding to do things God's way can be difficult. He'll help us make that choice if we ask.** Lead the children to ask God for direction

this week to be aware of times they've only wanted their own way.
- *Confess.* **Refusing to follow God is wrong. God wants to forgive us if we'll tell him we're sorry.** Allow children to confess when they've done wrong.
- *Thank.* **Think of the blessings you've had this week. Thank God for each one right now.**

Remember that no child should be forced to pray, but do encourage and invite each one. After you've said, "Amen," talk quietly with the children until the next activity.

StationMaster Card #6

This week your group learned from Luke 16 and Mark 1 that *our spirits need power food as much as our bodies do*. Lead your group in prayer in the following way.

- *Praise.* **Think of all God has given us for food to eat and for our spirits. Let's praise him for these things.** Lead the children in praising God for healthy foods, the Bible, music, worship, and other spiritual health builders.
- *Ask.* **Finding a snack when you're hungry isn't too hard most of the time. Let's ask God to show us how to feed our spirits every day too.** Model a prayer of request for spiritual food, then have children follow your example.

- *Confess.* **Can you think of times you've complained about what you eat? Have you forgotten to feed your spirit this week?** Lead children in prayers of confession for their wrong attitudes and lack of gratitude, as well as lack of attention to their spiritual care.
- *Thank.* **Take time now to thank God for all the good things he's blessed you with.** Encourage sentence prayers of thanks.

Remember that no child should be forced to pray, but do encourage and invite each one. After you've said, "Amen," talk quietly with the children until the next activity.

StationMaster Card #7

This week your group learned from Judges 6—7 and Numbers 13—14 that *God has my best in mind, even when things are hard*. Lead your group in prayer in the following way:

- *Praise.* **God never leaves us or gives up on us, even in the hard times.** Model for students praise to God for his faithfulness, understanding, care, gentleness, patience, and other attributes.
- *Ask.* **What is one tough thing you're dealing with right now? You can ask God to help you respond with a right attitude.** Lead children in asking God's help and ability to hang on.

- *Confess.* **It's easy to whine or complain when we're unhappy. But that isn't the best thing to do. You can let God know you're sorry if you've been feeling pity for yourself lately.**
- *Thank.* **Even when life is hard, there are things to be thankful for. What are they?** Encourage children to thank God for whatever they can think of.

Remember that no child should be forced to pray, but do encourage and invite each one. After you've said, "Amen," talk quietly with the children until the next activity.

StationMaster Card #8

This week your group learned from Acts 10 and Numbers 16 to *choose friends who honor God.* Lead your group in prayer in the following way:

■ *Praise.* **Jesus is the best friend we can have. Let's praise him for the ways he shows us friendship.** Lead the children in praising Jesus for various characteristics.

■ *Ask.* **Peter and Cornelius listened to God about who they should be friends with. Let's ask God for wisdom in choosing who to be friends with.** Allow children to pray for God's direction.

■ *Confess.* **Is there a friend who you need to apologize to? When we hurt someone's feelings or treat them wrongly, we need to ask their forgiveness.** Give children opportunity to tell God about a friendship problem and confess any wrong on their part.

■ *Thank.* **Friends are a gift. Let's thank God for our friends.** Allow children to give thanks for their friends by name if they choose.

Remember that no child should be forced to pray, but do encourage and invite each one. After you've said, "Amen," talk quietly with the children until the next activity.

StationMaster Card #9

This week your group learned from Matthew 20 and 2 Corinthians 11—12 that *happiness is being content with the life God gives me.* Lead your group in prayer in the following way:

■ *Praise.* **God is good to us no matter what our lives are like. He shows us mercy, kindness, and care in every situation.** Lead children in praising God for his goodness to them.

■ *Ask.* **God tells us to tell him how we feel. When we don't have an attitude of contentment, we can ask him to show us how to see our situation differently.** Encourage students to ask God for contentment with specific concerns and circumstances.

■ *Confess.* **How does our discontentment show up? With whining, complaining, grumpiness, and other bad attitudes. This is a chance for you to tell God you're sorry for any of those you've done this week.** Give students time to think about their attitudes this week and confess any wrong ones.

■ *Thank.* **Think about happy times this week. Have you thanked God for those yet?** Let children pray a sentence prayer of thanks.

Remember that no child should be forced to pray, but do encourage and invite each one. After you've said, "Amen," talk quietly with the children until the next activity.

StationMaster Card #10

This week your group learned from Numbers 12 and Esther 2—5, 8 that *the best place to be is under God's authority.* Lead your group in prayer in the following way:

- ■ *Praise.* **God is our perfect authority. He's always fair, loving, patient, and wise.** Lead children in praise for these and other attributes of God.
- ■ *Ask.* **It can be difficult to obey those in authority over us. Which authority do you need to do better at obeying and agreeing with?** Model for children a prayer asking God to change wrong thinking or actions.

- ■ *Confess.* **Just as Aaron admitted he and Miriam had done wrong, we need to admit when we have not been content to live under the authority God has put over us.** Encourage children to talk to God about times they have been rebellious or disobedient.
- ■ *Thank.* **Think about the adults in authority over you. Thank God for at least one of them.** Allow time for individual prayers of thanks.

Remember that no child should be forced to pray, but do encourage and invite each one. After you've said, "Amen," talk quietly with the children until the next activity.

StationMaster Card #11

This week your group learned from Nehemiah 5 and Luke 12 to be *willing to let go of whatever God has given you.* Lead your group in prayer in the following way:

- ■ *Praise.* **God is the source of everything we have. Let's praise God for generously giving us what we need and more.** Lead children in spontaneous prayers of praise.
- ■ *Ask.* **What might God be asking you to let go of? If you don't know, you can ask him to show you.** Allow time for children to talk with God and ask his direction about their possessions.

- ■ *Confess.* **Sometimes we envy the things others have, or wish we could have anything we want. Is that God's best for us? No way! Take a minute to tell God about wrong desires or envious feelings. He's ready to forgive you.**
- ■ *Thank.* **Instead of constantly asking for more, we can enjoy what we have and thank God for it.** Have students "count their blessings" and thank God for specific things he has given them.

Remember that no child should be forced to pray, but do encourage and invite each one. After you've said, "Amen," talk quietly with the children until the next activity.

StationMaster Card #12

This week your group learned from Daniel 3 and 2 Corinthians 10 to *praise God and not yourself.* Lead your group in prayer in the following way.

- *Praise.* **God is the one who most deserves our highest praise.** Have students praise God for being the one true God, for his truth, and other attributes they choose.
- *Ask.* **Do you run out of ways to praise God? The Holy Spirit helps us to pray as we should, so just ask him for ideas of how to give God the highest praise.** Give students time to talk to God and hear his voice.
- *Confess.* **We like to get praise, don't we? It's not wrong until we look for it and forget that God deserves more praise than we do.** Model a prayer of confession for a prideful or boasting spirit. Let children pray as they are led.
- *Thank.* **Aren't you glad we are children of the God who can protect us, even from a fiery furnace? Take time to thank God for the ways he has protected, helped, and given you power and strength this week.**

Remember that no child should be forced to pray, but do encourage and invite each one. After you've said, "Amen," talk quietly with the children until the next activity.

StationMaster Card #13

This week your group learned from Philippians 2 and Matthew 23 that *living for God is about serving, not being served.* Lead your group in prayer in the following way:

- *Praise.* **Praise Jesus for his love and care for us. He lived like a servant, and then was willing to die for us.** Give students opportunity to praise God for his great love and how they see it expressed in their lives.
- *Ask.* **Do you struggle with being a servant? God knows how we feel.** Lead students in asking God to change their hearts and attitudes.
- *Confess.* **There are times we know we should be serving others, but we choose to think of ourselves first.** Allow students to tell God when they've deliberately refused to serve or ignored someone's need.
- *Thank.* **We all have examples of good servants. Who can you think of who shows you how to serve like Jesus did? Lead students in prayers of thanksgiving for the good examples in their lives.**

Remember that no child should be forced to pray, but do encourage and invite each one. After you've said, "Amen," talk quietly with the children until the next activity.

On the Fast Track!

Prayer Challenge

Telling God you want to be more generous can be dangerous! God wants to hear you say you'll give up some things so others can be blessed. This week, tell God you want to share what he's given you. Ask him to show you who to be generous to.

Memory Verse

A generous man will prosper; he who refreshes others will himself be refreshed **(Proverbs 11:25).**
Note: Younger children may memorize the shorter version of this verse in **bold** *print.*

God gives me things so I can be generous with others.

Full of Blessings

Directions: Can you fill in the word below by writing or drawing things you have? Then thank God for his generosity in giving you so much.

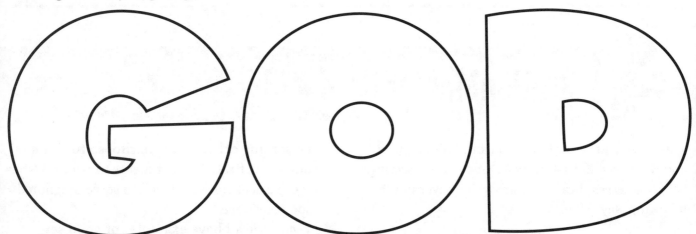

Your Turn

Your time is another way to be generous to others. Brainstorm with your family about a task or project you can do for someone else. Ideas: rake a neighbor's yard or pull weeds; play with a lonely child; help a teacher after school; wash an elderly person's car or windows.

Dear Parents and Guardians,
Please check off the items your child completed this week:

❑ Prayer Challenge
❑ Memory Verse
❑ Your Turn
❑ Full of Blessings

Adult Signature:
_____

FAST TRACK! TICKET

On the Fast Track!

Prayer Challenge

Praying God's own words in your prayers is powerful. This week, use Scripture in your prayers. Thank God that you are fearfully and wonderfully made by him, that his thoughts of you are so many you can't count them, and that he chose you to be his child and adopt you into his own family. Look up other Scriptures that express how you feel and pray them, too!

Memory Verse

Humble yourselves before the Lord, and he will lift you up (James 4:10).

Daniel 1; Acts 4:32—5:10

What God thinks of me is more important than what others think.

God Says

Decode this message:

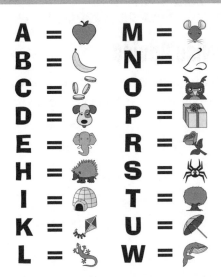

A = apple	M = mouse
B = banana	N = nose
C = pickle	O = owl
D = dog	P = present
E = elephant	R = rose
H = hedgehog	S = spider
I = igloo	T = tree
K = kite	U = umbrella
L = lizard	W = whale

Your Turn

Decide on a secret deed you can do for someone. You could do a brother's or sister's chore without telling anyone, clean up toys when it's not your turn, or anything else that will excite or help someone. Only God will know your good deed, and what God thinks about you is the most important opinion. How did it feel not to get thanks or approval from others for your good deed?

Dear Parents and Guardians,

Please check off the items your child completed this week:

- ❏ Prayer Challenge
- ❏ Memory Verse
- ❏ Your Turn
- ❏ God Says

Adult Signature:

_____

FAST TRACK! TICKET

On the Fast Track!

🙏 Prayer Challenge

What is one area that you have a hard time not being right? Do you argue or pout or try to prove you're right? This week, pray that God will show you as often as he needs to that you need his wisdom more than you need to be right. Thank him each day when you notice his answers to your prayers.

📖 Memory Verse

The fear of the Lord is the beginning of wisdom; all who follow his precepts have good understanding **(Psalm 111:10).** *Note: Younger children may memorize the shorter version of this verse in* **bold** *print.*

Genesis 4:1–12; 2 Chronicles 1:1–12

Having godly wisdom is better than being right all the time.

Wise Advice

Draw a picture or make a cartoon that illustrates the memory verse. Bring it to class next time.

Your Turn

Talk to an older person (like a grandparent or senior citizen neighbor) in person or by phone or e-mail about wisdom. Ask them for an example of how they learned or used wisdom in a real-time experience. Share their story with your family.

Dear Parents and Guardians,

Please check off the items your child completed this week:

- ❑ Prayer Challenge
- ❑ Memory Verse
- ❑ Your Turn
- ❑ Wise Advice

Adult Signature:

_____

FAST TRACK! TICKET

Prayer Challenge

Think about something that happened to you or someone you know that isn't fair. Instead of complaining or being angry or hurt, choose to pray about this unfair situation. Tell God about it and ask him to show you his justice in this situation.

Memory Verse

Blessed are they who maintain justice, who constantly do what is right (Psalm 106:3).

1 Samuel 2:12–17, 22–25, 27–35; 4:10–11; 1 Kings 3:16–28

God's justice shows me what is fair.

Matching

Match the person on one side with the description on the other side. Draw a line between them.

Eli	enemies of the Israelites
Eli's sons	wise king
Philistines	needed someone just to decide their argument
Solomon	priest of God
Two mothers	didn't obey God

Your Turn

Make up a short puppet skit about fairness and justice. Perform it for your family, some friends, your class at church, or some other group.

Dear Parents and Guardians,

Please check off the items your child completed this week:

- ☐ Prayer Challenge
- ☐ Memory Verse
- ☐ Your Turn
- ☐ Matching

Adult Signature: _____

FAST TRACK! TICKET

On the Fast Track!

Which Way? Maze

Directions: Will you choose God's way or your way? Find your way through the maze.

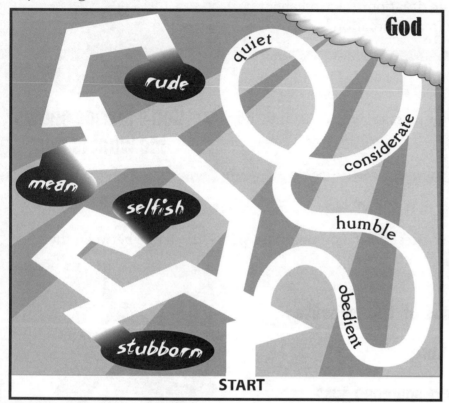

God

quiet

rude

considerate

mean

selfish

humble

stubborn

obedient

START

Your Turn

It's hard to let others have their way. Be on the lookout this week for opportunities to practice letting others have their way instead of trying to get them to do things your way.

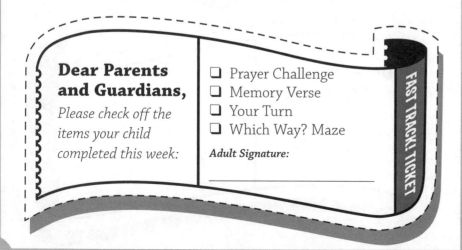

Dear Parents and Guardians,

Please check off the items your child completed this week:

- ❑ Prayer Challenge
- ❑ Memory Verse
- ❑ Your Turn
- ❑ Which Way? Maze

Adult Signature:

_____

FAST TRACK! TICKET

1 Samuel 15:1–23; Genesis 6:9–7:24

Choosing God's way is better than choosing my way.

Prayer Challenge

How can you know God's way? Ask God, and he'll tell you! Each day this week pray the words in Psalm 25:4–5. Pray with a parent or on your own. After you pray, be silent for at least a minute. God may start to show you his way—then, or later.

Memory Verse

Do nothing out of selfish ambition or vain conceit, **but in humility consider others better than yourselves.** Each of you should look not only to your own interests, but also to the interests of others **(Philippians 2:3-4).**

*Note: Younger children may memorize the shorter version of this verse in **bold** print.*

On the Fast Track!

Prayer Challenge

Talking to God and listening to him will feed your spirit with power food. Listening can be hard. Sometimes God doesn't seem to say anything. Just waiting and listening is hard to do. In your daily prayer time this week, spend as much time listening and waiting on God as you do talking.

Memory Verse

Jesus declared, **"I am the bread of life.** He who comes to me will never go hungry, and he who believes in me will never be thirsty" **(John 6:35).**

Note: Younger children may memorize the shorter version of this verse in **bold** *print.*

Health Food Fair

Use a highlighter to choose the healthy foods your body and your spirit need.

TV	fruit	jelly beans
Bible	worship	French fries
video game arcade	church	milk
singing praise songs	comic books	tuna
praying	cookies	

Write or draw your favorite spiritual power food:

Luke 16:19–31; Mark 1:4–8

Our spirits need power food as much as our bodies do.

Your Turn

People take vitamins to give their bodies extra strength, to keep from getting sick, and to have more energy. Make "spiritual" vitamins by taking copies of the memory verses you've been learning and rolling them up. Ask your mom, dad, or other adults at home to write down two or three verses too. Put these "spiritual vitamins" in a jar. Once a day, take a "spiritual vitamin" by choosing a rolled-up verse, reading it, and carrying it with you to remind you of what God says.

Dear Parents and Guardians,

Please check off the items your child completed this week:

- ❑ Prayer Challenge
- ❑ Memory Verse
- ❑ Your Turn
- ❑ Health Food Fair

Adult Signature:

_____

FAST TRACK! TICKET

On the Fast Track!

Prayer Challenge

Talking to God about what's hard in your life is a good thing. But God doesn't want to hear whining! He's interested in your feelings, your needs, and your problems. Practice telling him what's going on—without complaining. If things are good in your life, pray for someone who is having a hard time right now.

Memory Verse

Come near to God and he will come near to you (James 4:8).

God has my best in mind, even when things are hard.

Gideon Gets through It

Put these events from the story about Gideon in the right order by writing "1" by the first thing that happened, "2" by the next thing, and so on. Then read Judges 6 and 7 with your family to see how well you did.

_____ **An angel told Gideon God wanted him to become the leader of the Israelites.**

_____ **The Midianites ran away, and the Israelites were free again.**

_____ **The Israelites blew trumpets and broke jars.**

_____ **The Israelites had a hard life because their enemies, the Midianites, kept attacking them.**

_____ **God told Gideon when to attack the enemy because he was giving Gideon the victory.**

[ANSWERS: 2, 5, 4, 1, 3]

Your Turn

Trusting that God has your best in mind is like scraping rust off a tool or using a rock tumbler to make a rock into a shiny gem. The hard thing turns the object into something better. Ask a parent for a job like scrubbing a pan, scraping mud off boots, or polishing silver. The work is hard and slow. But the thing you're working on will be clean and much better when you finish. That's what God can do when you're going through a hard time.

Dear Parents and Guardians,
Please check off the items your child completed this week:

❏ Prayer Challenge
❏ Memory Verse
❏ Your Turn
❏ Gideon Gets through It

Adult Signature:

_____

FAST TRACK! TICKET

Prayer Challenge

To be a good friend, pray for your friends. Ask them what they need prayer for, and pray about their need all week. Tell your friends one way to pray for you. Try praying with a friend once this week.

Acts 10; Numbers 16:1–35

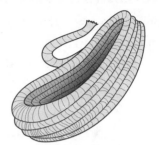

Choose friends who honor God.

Memory Verse

A righteous man is cautious in friendship, but the way of the wicked leads them astray (Proverbs 12:26).

Friendship Cartoon

Draw a cartoon about friendship. Use the boxes below. You could also make up your own cartoon.

Moe and Joe were good friends.	Moe came up with a plan. "Let's _____," he said. But it wasn't a good idea.	"I don't think we should do that!" said Joe. "Instead, let's _____."	So the friends _____. Moe was glad Joe was a friend who wanted to honor God.

Your Turn

Read or ask your parent to read to you a book or story about something that honors God. Then share the book with a friend. Read it together, or have an adult read it with you and your friend. Ask that friend to share the book with another friend.

Dear Parents and Guardians,

Please check off the items your child completed this week:

❑ Prayer Challenge
❑ Memory Verse
❑ Your Turn
❑ Friendship Cartoon

Adult Signature:

_____

FAST TRACK! TICKET

On the Fast Track!

Travel toward Contentment

Following Jesus is the start to a life of joy and contentment. Pretend you and Jesus are walking this maze together. Collect the letters as you go. What do they spell?

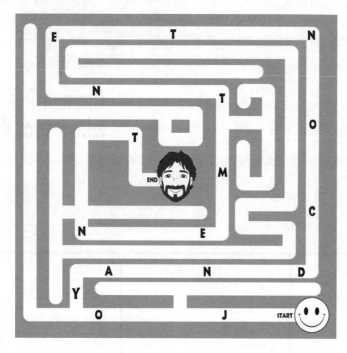

Matthew 20:1–15;
2 Corinthians
11:24–33; 12:8–10

Happiness is being content with the life God gives me.

Prayer Challenge

This week when you pray, instead of asking for things, just be thankful. Thank God for specific things: your family, friends, your home, the good qualities God has made in you. When you feel the urge to be disappointed or unhappy with your life, say a sentence prayer of thanks for something. God will change your attitude when you choose to be content instead of unhappy.

Your Turn

Give joy this week. Be someone's secret friend. Do nice things for that person, like leave a note with a compliment or smiley face. Do a chore for them, but don't tell it was you. Give them a little gift, like some gum or a handmade card. While you're busy sharing joy with someone, you will become more content with your own life.

Memory Verse

You have made known to me the path of life; **you will fill me with joy in your presence,** with eternal pleasures at your right hand **(Psalm 16:11).** *Note: Younger children may memorize the shorter version of this verse in **bold** print.*

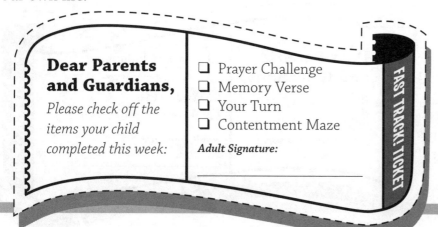

Dear Parents and Guardians,

Please check off the items your child completed this week:

- ☐ Prayer Challenge
- ☐ Memory Verse
- ☐ Your Turn
- ☐ Contentment Maze

Adult Signature:

FAST TRACK! TICKET

On the Fast Track!

Numbers 12; Esther 2:15–20; 3:6–9; 4:7–14; 5:1–2; 8:1–8

Prayer Challenge

Think about the people in charge of you: parents, teachers, older brothers and sisters, coaches, babysitter. Pray for the people in authority over you, that they will be wise and fair. Pray to have a willing and cheerful attitude toward them.

The best place to be is under God's authority.

Memory Verse

Trust in the LORD with all your heart and lean not on your own understanding; in all your ways acknowledge him, and he will make your paths straight **(Proverbs 3:5–6).**

Note: Younger children may memorize the shorter version of this verse in **bold** *print.*

Your Turn

Play a game with a child younger than you. Let her be in charge of starting the game, deciding on the rules, and choosing things. This is good practice for you in obeying and following those in authority. You also are giving a good example to the younger kids playing with you.

Under the Umbrella

Draw a picture of yourself under an umbrella. Write the people in authority over you on the umbrella (don't forget God!).

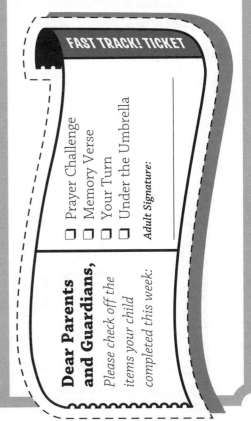

FAST TRACK! TICKET

☐ Prayer Challenge
☐ Memory Verse
☐ Your Turn
☐ Under the Umbrella

Adult Signature: _____

Dear Parents and Guardians,
Please check off the items your child completed this week:

On the Fast Track!

Consider the Lilies

Directions: Circle the things that are part of the words Jesus gave us in Luke 12:22–34.

Your Turn

If you made a box to collect things you can share or give away, start collecting this week. To make a "Hold It Lightly" box, decorate a large box or bag. Use it to collect things you sense God is asking you to let go of: things to give to someone who needs it more than you do, or as a place to collect new things to donate or share (school supplies, craft items, sports cards, pet goods).

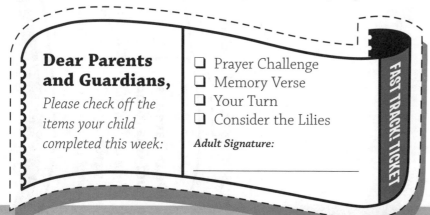

Dear Parents and Guardians,

Please check off the items your child completed this week:

- ❏ Prayer Challenge
- ❏ Memory Verse
- ❏ Your Turn
- ❏ Consider the Lilies

Adult Signature:

_____

FAST TRACK! TICKET

Nehemiah 5:1–13; Luke 12:22–34

Be willing to let go of whatever God has given you.

🙏 Prayer Challenge

Most people in the world have much less than we do in North America. Choose a missionary, foreign family overseas, foster child, or another person/family who lives with much less than you do. Pray all week for God to supply their needs. Ask him if he wants you to help them in any way.

📖 Memory Verse

Do not set your heart on what you will eat or drink; do not worry about it. **But seek his kingdom,** and these things will be given to you as well (Luke 12:29, 31).

*Note: Younger children may memorize the shorter version of this verse in **bold** print.*

Prayer Challenge

Make praising God your main way of praying this week. Praise him for something different each time. Ask an adult for ideas if you run out. See how many things you can praise God for.

Memory Verse

Great is the LORD and most worthy of praise; his greatness no one can fathom (Psalm 145:3).

Note: Younger children may memorize the shorter version of this verse in **bold** *print.*

Daniel 3:1, 8–26; 2 Corinthians 10:12–18

Praise God, not yourself.

Praise Words

Unscramble the words to reveal things about who God is and what he does that you can praise him for.

1. siwe   _ _ _ _
2. stuj   _ _ _ _
3. ruecilmf   _ _ _ _ _ _ _ _
4. iorgvnifg   _ _ _ _ _ _ _ _ _
5. vloe   _ _ _ _
6. lruopefw   _ _ _ _ _ _ _ _
7. treag   _ _ _ _ _

Your Turn

When people do something special they get an award. Make a simple trophy that honors God for all the great things he is. Use whatever you have at home (paper and cardboard, recycled materials, clay, craft foam, etc.). Put the trophy in your room to remember that if you want to boast, boast in the Lord as Paul did.

Dear Parents and Guardians,

Please check off the items your child completed this week:

- ❏ Prayer Challenge
- ❏ Memory Verse
- ❏ Your Turn
- ❏ Praise Words

Adult Signature:

_____

FAST TRACK! TICKET

ANSWERS: 1. WISE 2. JUST 3. MERCIFUL 4. FORGIVING 5. LOVE 6. POWERFUL 7. GREAT

On the Fast Track!

Prayer Challenge

If you truly want to live for God, ask him daily who you can serve. You will be surprised at who God brings to you to serve. Keep praying to have a love for serving like Jesus did.

Memory Verse

For even the Son of Man did not come to be served, but to serve, and to give his life as a ransom for many (Mark 10:45).

*Note: Younger children may memorize the shorter version of this verse in **bold** print.*

Philippians 2:3–11; Matthew 23:1–11

Living for God is about serving, not being served.

The Meaning of Serving

What does a servant do? Use the letters of "SERVE" below to start words or sentences that make a description of a servant.

S _____

E _____

R _____

V _____

E _____

Your Turn

Choose one way to serve at home. Make it something that no one else would choose to do. Decide to serve in that way at least this week, and longer. Don't do it for anyone's praise or thanks, but just to practice serving the way Jesus did. How does it feel?

Dear Parents and Guardians,

Please check off the items your child completed this week:

❑ Prayer Challenge
❑ Memory Verse
❑ Your Turn
❑ The Meaning of Serving

Adult Signature:

_____

FAST TRACK! TICKET